MARK RAYCROFT
PILI PALM-LEIS

MW00335676

CARIBOU

Wind Walkers of the Northern Wilderness

FIREFLY BOOKS

A FIREFLY BOOK

Published by Firefly Books Ltd. 2022

Copyright © 2022 Firefly Books Ltd.

Text copyright © 2022 Mark Raycroft and Pili Palm-Leis

Photos copyright © 2022 Mark Raycroft Photography Inc., unless noted

All rights reserved. No part of this publication may be reproduced, stored in a retrieval system, or transmitted in any form or by any means, electronic, mechanical, photocopying, recording or otherwise, without the prior written permission of the Publisher.

First printing

Library of Congress Control Number: 2022934052

Library and Archives Canada Cataloguing in Publication
Title: Caribou : wind walkers of the northern wilderness / Mark Raycroft, Pili Palm-Leis.
Names: Raycroft, Mark, author, photographer. | Palm-Leis, Pili, author.
Description: First edition. | Includes bibliographical references and index.
Identifiers: Canadiana 20220188092 | ISBN 9780228103974 (softcover)
Subjects: LCSH: Caribou. | LCSH: Caribou—Ecology. | LCSH: Caribou—Pictorial works.
Classification: LCC QL737.U55 R39 2022 | DDC 599.65/80222—dc23

Published in the United States by
Firefly Books (U.S.) Inc.
P.O. Box 1338, Ellicott Station
Buffalo, New York 14205

Published in Canada by
Firefly Books Ltd.
50 Staples Avenue, Unit 1
Richmond Hill, Ontario L4B 0A7

Cover and interior design: Stacey Cho

Printed in China

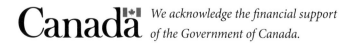

We acknowledge the financial support of the Government of Canada.

BIBLIOGRAPHY

MARKRAYCROFTWILDPHOTO

ACKNOWLEDGMENTS

There are many people to whom I wish to extend a heartfelt "Thank you!"

To the love of my life, my wife Pili: Thank you for sharing in so many adventures across this amazing planet! Your research and writing collaboration on this project was greatly appreciated. You've always been my strongest supporter — here's to future explorations!

To my wonderful children, Martha and Andrew: Thank you for sharing in many adventures as well! You have both experienced caribou country, a treasure that I was delighted to share with you. Andrew, your photography skills continue to impress!

To my parents, Gerry and Sheryl Raycroft: Thank you for introducing me to the wonders of the outdoors. You were both extremely supportive and always encouraged me to follow my dreams.

To my many friends who have shared in wilderness adventures: Dolf DeJong, Jason Griffiths, Luke Vander Vennen, Eric and Debbie Brewer, Darren Raycroft, Bill Gadzos, Bob Schillereff, Jake Vanderzwet, Jeff Raycroft, Don Kesler, Joey Olivieri, Yaron Eini, Tyler Burr, Ron Hayes, Michael Mauro, Missy MacKenzie, Jason Loftus, Simone Heinrich and Jeanette Fraser. Thank you to Dr. Gabriela Mastromonaco for taking the time to talk with me about her visionary work, which is so critical for the preservation of genetic biodiversity of threatened wildlife species.

To the wonderful people at Minden Pictures: Larry Minden, Stacy Frank, Chris Carey, Catherine Converse and Steve Phillips.

And a special thank you to the talented team at Firefly Books for making this book possible: Lionel Koffler, Julie Takasaki, Stacey Cho and Darcy Shea.

And, last but definitely not least, all of the caribou from Alaska through to Newfoundland that have allowed me to walk the tundra with you. Thank you for the many unforgettable moments!

CONTENTS

IN THE COMPANY OF CARIBOU

The tallest snow-capped peaks in North America rose above the fiery red tundra as we camped in the heart of Alaska. The remote wilderness of Denali National Park and Preserve was to be our home for the next two weeks.

A few days into September, the autumn colors were at their peak, and the winds and rains had held off. My friend Bob and I welcomed another day of hiking and scouting the taiga, hoping our efforts would result in finding grand examples of megafauna to photograph in this incredible landscape.

The vastness of this region is a challenge to describe in words. The miles-wide valley floor and low-lying foothills seem like they'd be easy to traverse, but one quickly realizes the effort and focus required to navigate this terrain.

You'd expect to catch a glimpse of animals if you just climbed high enough, but the landscape does not always reveal its true nature, nor the wildlife it conceals. Numerous valleys and ponds are hidden by the rolling

Clash of the northern titans!

6

hills and wherever the elevation changes, which is as frequently as every hundred yards or so, impenetrable willow brush sprouts up to consume most slopes.

Following our strategy, we hiked to an elevated knoll to glass the surrounding miles of wilderness. The fiery red leaves of the frost-laden berry bushes created a surreal canvas for photography.

We'd sit and scan for half an hour, hoping for a flash of antler or for our eyes to spot the flicker of movement as a caribou, moose, bear or wolf moved across the seemingly endless taiga.

On this day, it didn't take long to catch a glimpse of a crown of bone. Antlers! Caribou! Careful observation revealed a bachelor group of nine magnificent caribou bulls about 500 yards away. My heart skipped a beat.

The scene was stunning. You could almost believe that the caribou hadn't changed in millennia in these ancient ranges, as if time had stopped in this vast valley. The ancestors of these animals walked these very same paths.

A trio of barren-ground caribou bulls feed in the Alaskan wilderness.

Opposite: I never tire of this view. A handsome caribou, a raven and Mount Denali help to put what's important in life into perspective.

A tundra walker in his element.

Opposite: A picture-perfect pose from a stunning monarch!

The bulls were feeding and didn't seem to be in a hurry to go anywhere as Bob and I planned our approach. We would keep the wind in our favor as we neared the group.

It wasn't far before we were challenged with plotting a course through a dense patch of willows. This grove was too long to travel around and only about 60 yards wide. Bob was still assembling his pack, so I entered the labyrinth first, thinking I'd find a game trail through the 15-foot-tall thickets that would spill us out closer to the caribou. Luck was on my side, as I readily found a decent path. The animals know the best route, the path of least resistance.

Before entering any thick vegetation in the Far North, I always take a moment to talk fairly loudly to myself and continue my monologue until I'm in the clear, especially in the heart of grizzly country. The last thing that I want to do is startle a sleeping bear. At this point, I was too far away for my chatter to be noticed by the caribou.

In fact, we wanted the caribou to see us and be aware of our presence — just not to smell us at the same time. By seeing us from a greater distance, it would give them more time to realize that we weren't predators. This doesn't always work, but when it does, the caribou relax and resume their natural behavior.

As I maneuvered through the willows, I noticed an oval depression in the vegetation. I continued talking aloud to myself to let any animals in the vicinity know that I was there. (I told a good tale, to be sure.) I didn't pay much attention to the flattened mat of grass, as it was empty and could've been made days ago. It might have been a bear, but maybe a moose bedded there. After 10 minutes, I exited the willows and walked another 80 yards to the far side of the open plateau to check on the caribou and wait for Bob.

A few minutes later, he emerged from the thicket, but from a different trail. When he stepped out, he just stopped and stared at me with a confused look on his face. Curious, I waited for him to catch up. He declared that I must have been

in there walking right beside him — he'd heard something moving through the shrubbery nearby and had assumed it was me! Our guess was that my non-stop talking had roused a grizzly into leaving his daybed and heading in the direction where Bob was working through the brambles. It must've passed close to him … closer than Bob wanted.

Thankfully, the bear avoided him and moved on. We never saw that particular bruin, which was fine with us. We always carry bear spray on these wilderness trips, as grizzlies make daily appearances in this region, but we'd prefer to avoid these mountain bears while on foot.

We joked about the close encounter as we pressed on together toward the band of caribou, calmly grazing at the next rise.

As we circled around to remain downwind, Mount Denali presented a stunning opportunity for an environmental portrait to illustrate the grandeur of this wild place that these caribou call home. At one point, a raven flew over one of the bulls, calling and sharing its thoughts on the day.

Every hundred yards or so we would stop, recompose and photograph the animals again. On this day, our measured approach was successful.

Opposite: When autumn colors and caribou come together.

One of the bulls thrashing an evergreen, putting his velvet-free antlers to use and expressing dominance toward the other males in the vicinity.

A majestic barren-ground caribou bull poses on an autumn ridge in Alaska.

Opposite: Happy Bou? He may have been, but his smile was mostly the result of panting after an energetic sparring match with another bull.

The next few hours were a whirlwind of photography. We were able to capture two bulls sparring and bulls thrashing willows with their antlers, feeding, bedding, even stretching after being bedded. One handsome fellow offered us a series of snapshots where he appears to be laughing, but he was in fact panting after a sparring bout with another stag.

Each bull's antlers were unique and beautifully branched, which made picture taking incredible at every angle. Photographing any two ungulates sparring is exciting but challenging. The action can be fast and intense. Trying to keep the image in focus, having the correct camera settings and composition, and timing the shots so that the bulls' eyes are clear of vegetation or body parts are tests of one's camera skills. Thankfully, we both came away that day with excellent results.

On top of all this, these bulls were all in great condition, as it was only a matter of weeks before rutting activity would ramp up. One of them had the whitest, most perfect mane that I had ever seen — a truly stunning specimen!

After their exertions, a pair of them bedded down in an ideal location to make it look like they were peeking over a knoll — concealed, but with their tall crowns giving them away. They weren't trying to hide from us, as we were only 60 yards from where they laid down, but the composition remains one of my favorites.

I will never forget or cease being grateful for the views and experiences that unfolded beneath the might and majesty of Denali that day. As wildlife photographers, we never know what awaits us when we venture into the wild. Sometimes

14

the animals are a no-show. Sometimes they are content to play out the day obscured by willows or other photographic obstacles. Then there's the weather, which can change surprisingly fast in caribou country — especially in the mountains. But on this day, the stars aligned and offered us a remarkable encounter with a bachelor group of photogenic wind walkers of the northern wilderness.

Studying and photographing the antlered creatures of our continent has been a lifelong passion and a huge part of my 30-year career as a wildlife photographer. Each journey to the land of caribou has been a thrilling and unique adventure. It's a tremendously different environment than the one where most people lead their day-to-day lives. In caribou country, nature still rules, and these magnificent, crowned mammals roam as they have since the last Ice Age.

Across the continent, from the rugged northern wilds of Alaska to the barrens of Newfoundland, the dozens of trips that we've shared in the company of caribou have taught us so much about this species and their integral part on this planet. We hope that you enjoy the images and stories from these expeditions and that this book will transport you to the Far North, to the wondrous land of the caribou.

A pair of bulls bed down nearby. It was as though they were hiding, which really wasn't the case — especially not with those antlers!

A BRIEF HISTORY

The story of contemporary caribou begins during the last Ice Age, over two million years ago. With huge quantities of water frozen in ice, the sea levels had receded, exposing land bridges between continents. Pleistocene-era reindeer could walk unhindered from mainland Europe to the British Isles. Millions of these majestically antlered herbivores also migrated freely across the ephemeral tracts of land between Asia and the Americas, roaming North America's snow fields with mammoth and mastodon. Ancient caribou grazed on primordial lichens and marched through their annual cycles of migration, breeding and calving, impervious to the cold that would continue to grip the land for thousands of years. The caribou that emerged on the other side of the glacial epoch were creatures forged by snow and ice.

The caribou that wander North America today evolved in Beringia, the land and maritime region between Russia and Canada. As the glacial ice shelves melted for the last time, the Bering Land Bridge disappeared beneath the sea, and the vast herds became separated. The caribou of North America and the reindeer of Eurasia are still the same species and could interbreed given the opportunity.

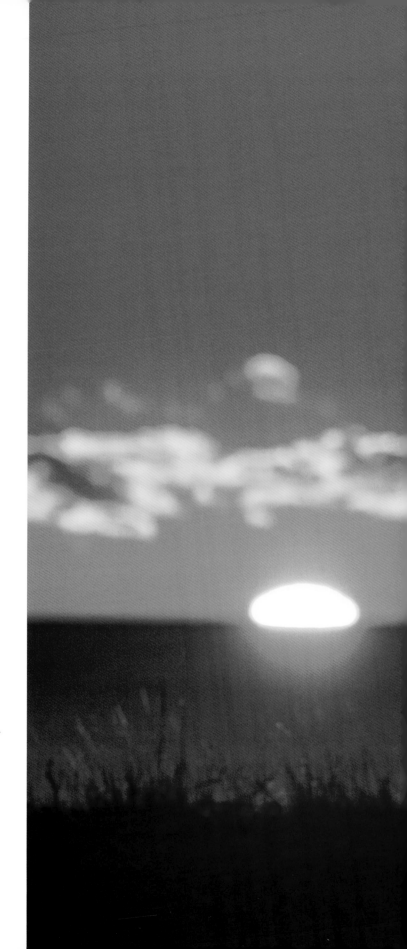

Much of the landscape in caribou country has remained the same for millennia. The supermoon crests the Alaska Range.

Opposite: A stunning example of a mature caribou bull in the evening glow on the tundra.

But caribou have remained wild and free on this continent, while most reindeer have been integrated into ancient human herding culture through various degrees of domestication. The oldest Canadian caribou fossils date back 1.2 million years.

Found throughout the circumpolar North, from Scandinavia to Greenland, caribou and reindeer formed the basis of most Arctic and subarctic cultures. Most human life in the north would not have been possible without caribou. Indigenous peoples of the past depended on caribou for the necessities of life: meat; fat for light and cooking; hides for tents, clothing and footwear; bone for needles, scrapers, fishhooks and a variety of weapons and tools.

The remains of caribou accompany most Paleolithic dwelling sites in Europe, including those of the Neanderthals over 40,000 years ago. Early hunters depended on caribou coming to them, and ancient settlements were constructed along caribou and reindeer migration routes. Back then, there were no airplanes to scout out the approaching herds and confirm their imminent arrival. If Indigenous

peoples didn't intercept the caribou in transit, many faced starvation. That interdependency is important to this present day.

If more proof is required that caribou have been significant to humans from time immemorial, one need only view photos of the oldest known paintings in the world. The stunning 30,000-year-old murals decorating the Chauvet-Pont-d'Arc Cave in southeast France include a rock face entitled *The Reindeer Panel*, with graceful depictions of Ice Age *Rangifer tarandus* (in motion, naturally), unmistakable thanks to their forward-sweeping antlers and distinctive brow tines or "shovels."

A wide-antlered bull caribou in early autumn.
PHOTO CREDIT: ANDREW RAYCROFT

Caribou are the most northerly of all domesticated animals. Reindeer were first tamed about 5,000 years ago by the Indigenous peoples of the Altai Mountains, which separate Russia and Mongolia. For millennia, semi-nomadic reindeer herders in the region have lived in close contact with their animals, milking the reindeer, using them as pack and draft animals and riding them to muster the herd. Over time, the practice of reindeer husbandry selected particular traits such as calmness and certain coat colors. The contemporary Tsaatan (Dukha) peoples of northern Mongolia still depend on their domesticated reindeer for food, transportation and even tourism. In exchange, the reindeer are protected from predators and enjoy the care and attention of the community. They are also tightly woven into the ritual fabric of the culture. At birth, every child is given a white reindeer as their totemic animal.

Recent discoveries at archeological sites in northern Siberia offer a window into ancient reindeer-taming methods. A University of Alberta scientist working at a dig above the Arctic Circle unearthed parts of an artifact that appeared to be a reindeer harness. Present-day Siberian reindeer herders identified the 2,000-year-old remnants as a training harness for young reindeer. The curved, cut sections of antler, carved with barbs on the inside, would be fastened around the animal's head to discourage resistance.

Opposite: An iconic woodland caribou on alert.

In North America, there is archeological evidence linking people and caribou as far back as 25,000 years ago. So intertwined were the lives of caribou and humans that, even in legends, the fate of caribou will also be the fate of their human brothers and sisters. Today, caribou are still one of the most significant wildlife species for northern First Nations.

Historically, Indigenous hunters mainly speared migrating caribou as they crossed waterways. They would lie in wait, their kayaks hidden in the willows along the shore, until the lead animals, hesitating on the bank, succumbed to the enormous pressure of thousands of caribou bodies pushing from behind. Once the herd was committed, the caribou would stream into lakes or rivers without pause. At this moment, when the caribou could not flee or even turn back, the hunters would paddle close and spear the animals. A hunting group could harvest many animals quickly, as the carcasses would simply float downstream in the current and could be recovered later on.

Other techniques employed by early northern hunters included running caribou off of rocky outcrops and dispatching the injured animals. In the case of woodland

Reindeer entering yurt for food, Khovsgol, Mongolia.
PHOTO CREDIT: JAMI TARRIS/MINDEN PICTURES

herds, humans funneled caribou into corrals through handmade drive lanes of brush or stone. Computer simulations of ancient caribou herd movements help archeologists to decide where to look for fossil evidence of caribou hunting. The simulations can highlight critical migratory choke points in the area.

It is at one of these predicted choke points that the remarkably intact remnants of a prehistoric kill site was discovered, preserved for 9,000 years in the waters of Lake Huron. Ten thousand years ago, the Laurentide Ice Sheet extended north from the top of Lake Superior to Greenland. The colossal runoff from melting Ice Age glaciers had not yet filled the Great Lakes to their current capacity.

Ontario was part of the caribou spring and fall migration route as the animals skirted the edges of the ice fortress in the north. The resident Stone Age hunters, working cooperatively with other families, anticipated the appearance of the caribou herds and constructed a drive lane at the choke point with rocks piled into parallel berms. V-shaped blinds

A mature caribou bull crosses the barrens.

were set up along the chute to hide from the approaching animals. As soon as the herd had passed, women and children would emerge from the blinds, forcing the caribou to continue in the direction of the corral. The caribou would be trapped.

So critical were the caribou for survival that Indigenous tribes all along the caribou corridor collaborated to share whatever game was taken. In this way, if the herd veered off course, there was a chance that someone in the cooperative hunting network would encounter caribou. The fortunate community would harvest much more than they required and share the game with others, in the knowledge that their families might be the next ones in need.

CARIBOU ECOLOGY

Caribou endure. The Arctic, where they roam, is scoured and pummeled by rain, snow and winds that shear off of the world's largest oceans. Cold, churning rivers fed from alpine glaciers repeatedly cut across migration routes. Year after year, caribou return to this unforgiving land that hardens like stone during winter and revives during spring in fits of rushing water and swarms of ravenous insects. For the legendary herds that call this fearsome domain home, however, it's just another day.

The word caribou is derived from the Mi'kmaq word *xalibu* or *Qalipu*, which aptly means "the one who paws or shovels snow." The Latin name for caribou, *Rangifer tarandus*, means a deer from the Arctic and subarctic regions. Caribou and reindeer, their Eurasian counterparts, belong to the family *Cervidae*, even-toed, hooved ungulates that include moose, elk, mule deer and white-tailed deer. The distinguishing features of this family include a four-chambered stomach and the ability to shed and regrow antlers on an annual basis.

Caribou are built for survival in the Far North. A herd waits out a snowstorm near Goose Bay, Labrador, Canada.
PHOTO CREDIT: NIGEL BEAN/MINDEN PICTURES

Cervids have much in common, but only caribou have developed the extraordinary and complex physical adaptations required for life commuting around the North Pole. Caribou have nothing to fear from the cold; it is a friend and protector to them. It is because of the harsh elements in caribou country that they have been largely left undisturbed, a singular blessing for animals that are dependent on uninterrupted access to vast tracts of pristine land.

From the tips of their toes to the ends of their nose, caribou have evolved to survive and thrive in one of the world's most inhospitable places. In the most northerly of caribou ranges, the temperature can reach -45°C and stay there for days or weeks at a time.

A caribou's winter fur is typically a lighter shade of grey or brown and, like the pelage of other Arctic species such as wolves and musk oxen, is composed of two distinct layers: a curly, highly insulating undercoat, which hugs the body, and an overcoat of long, stiff hairs, which stand out to block strong winds and shed snow. The light, protective guard hairs, full of air pockets, are the caribou equivalent of a puffer jacket and a life jacket in one, keeping the animals warm, but also buoyant when swimming in open water.

Aside from moose, caribou are the only member of the deer family with fully furred heads, including extra fur around their compact ears and dense hair on their muzzles. With insulated noses to reduce frost buildup, caribou use their keen sense of smell to detect vegetation and are constantly rooting through the snow for food. Caribou nasal passages are also covered with fine, short bristles that warm the frigid air before it's inhaled. This same system captures condensed air when they exhale, feeding the moisture back into the body. Caribou also conserve water through the winter by urinating less.

Caribou are stockier than their moose and deer cousins. Their shorter legs lose very little heat due to a dense microcirculation of arteries and veins that absorbs

the heat from the blood before it enters the extremities and returns it to the blood as it reenters the body. The normal body temperature of caribou is 38.8°C and their legs are a cool 7.7°C.

Caribou and reindeer hooves act as multipurpose tools for tackling the challenging terrain they encounter as they navigate the changing seasons. In spring, their hooves fill out into spongy pads, increasing the surface area of their footprint and enabling caribou to float across boggy ground.

Caribou have fully furred heads, including extra fur around their compact ears and dense hair on their muzzles to withstand the elements on the tundra.

29

A bull, cow and calf all line up — perfectly displaying the differences in their size.

Opposite: Caribou have evolved hooves that transform throughout the seasons to adjust to the extreme changes in their environment.

Caribou feet are the widest of all deer. A large male can leave a track as big as 5" x 8". They may be the marathoners in the deer family, but caribou can run fast, even across frozen lakes. Their primary defense against predators is to flee, which they do at speeds of up to 50 kilometers per hour (kmph). If caribou do fall through thin ice, their lower center of gravity and uniquely shaped toes make it possible for them to climb back out. No other member of the deer family would be capable of this feat.

The caribou's large, paddle-like feet also make them excellent swimmers. Adults are known to swim as fast as 6 kmph, and even 2-month-old calves have been recorded swimming over a mile as the herd moves between islands.

As winter approaches, caribou hooves grow harder and longer, and the soft pads contract into tough concave cups. When the large, curved front toes and the well-developed dew claws spread apart, caribou feet become effective snowshoes. The coarse hair between the toes lengthens to protect the pads from abrasion and provide better traction on ice. Eventually, the hair covers everything except the horny rim of the hoof.

Sharp-edged winter hooves offer stable support as caribou traverse frozen lakes and negotiate snowdrifts packed as hard as cement. As they endlessly journey across the north, the tendons of their feet slip over the bones beneath, causing the hooves to "click" with every step. This adaptation helps the herds stay together when visibility is low due to snow or fog.

Their sharp feet can also be formidable weapons of defense, but the most important job of winter hooves is to dig food "craters" in the snow and expose the

Opposite: Caribou can run at speeds of up to 50 kmph, and this young bull looks like he's enjoying the exercise!

Caribou are strong swimmers, thanks to their paddle-like hooves.

A female caribou feeds on lichen along the northern coastline.

Opposite, left: A close-up of reindeer moss, or caribou moss, which is actually a species of lichen.

Opposite, right: A young male munches mouthfuls of lichen, storing energy for the approaching winter.

lichens and dry sedges essential to the caribou's survival. To deal with the scarcity of forage during the winter months, a caribou's metabolic rate drops by 25 percent. Because they burn less calories, they can subsist on less food.

With one abundant species known as "reindeer moss," lichen is the staple food of a caribou's diet. It is the key to winter survival for the wild species in both North America and Eurasia. Lichens are not plants. They are a composite organism of algae and fungi in a symbiotic relationship. The algae create energy from photosynthesis, and the fungi provide the support structure. These unique characteristics allow lichen to withstand extreme cold and droughts. It is found year-round in every range — on rocks, hanging from tree branches and covering frozen soil — and the abundance of lichen is directly linked to the abundance of caribou.

Although long-lived, lichen is fragile. It has no roots, absorbing water and minerals from the environment, and, in the Arctic, grows a mere quarter of an inch a year. Fortunately, the caribou's wandering ways protect the vital algae/fungi hybrid from being overbrowsed. With their superb sense of smell, caribou can locate lichen even under a foot of snow. Typically poor in nutritional value, lichen needs to be consumed in large quantities to keep caribou in good condition — about 3 kilograms daily in the winter. To compensate for this high-carb, low-protein diet, caribou actually "recycle" the urea that is a by-product of their metabolism. This unique adaptation helps them extract every last bit of nourishment from their food. Fermentation, as a natural part of a ruminant's digestive process, helps to keep caribou bodies warm.

Rumination is a two-stage process which involves tearing vegetation and swallowing it almost whole. When caribou find a safe place to rest, they regurgitate this partially digested cud, grinding it thoroughly between their back molars. During rumination, caribou will snatch brief naps, either lying down or standing with their eyes closed, heads swaying slightly.

A cow and her calf rest mid-morning to chew their cud. It was breezy that day, so I missed the inside joke.

At these moments in the daily foraging cycle, caribou are vulnerable. Animals that roam densely wooded habitats, either alone or in small groups, will ruminate in the concealment of the forest. Larger herds will find open bogs or frozen lakes and lie together with their eyes pointed in many directions. Caribou notice the slightest movements and can see a broad spectrum of light, including ultraviolet, which helps them detect lichen amid the white snow. Their UV vision also highlights the outline of predators and where they have urinated.

On one of our trips, a few years ago, we were hoping to capture footage of barren-ground caribou in Alaska and not having much luck. Unlike other years where the bulls had been very tolerant of human presence, the animals in the region where we were hiking seemed inexplicably nervous. We knew that the arrival of grizzlies in an area always made caribou jumpy, and we were aware of at

36

least one that was hanging around. Perhaps a pack of wolves had recently passed through and run them, testing the bulls for weakness. Either way, when we spotted an animal or two and attempted to approach, they were uncharacteristically shy.

Then our luck seemed to change. We found a very impressive lone bull and worked our way up through the thick ground cover until we were parallel to him. I managed to capture a few images from a distance, but since we were still well over a hundred yards away, even my 500mm lens wasn't cutting it. As we slowly got closer, the bull went behind taller vegetation, and we lost sight of him.

We paused for a few minutes and then stepped clear of the tall brush, only to notice that he'd covered quite a bit of ground and was already a couple of hundred yards below. Staying in sight, he allowed us to get within 80 yards while he fed and occasionally looked up.

Then he did something that I'd never seen a caribou do before. Facing away, he reared up like a horse with his front hooves in the air! When he came down, he ran for a hundred yards. He then glanced back and resumed feeding while slowly meandering away. At the time, I was unsure what caused the elaborate display. I assumed that it was a botfly, the sound of which can immediately send a caribou into a panicked gallop.

An alarmed caribou rears up. Sometimes caribou, in rearing up, release a warning pheromone to alert other caribou as well.

It wasn't until later that I heard that caribou have small scent glands, located behind the legs where the ankle meets the hoof, which secrete a "warning" chemical. When caribou feel threatened, they kick out with a back leg or rear up to release the pheromone to alert others.

I regret that we may have elicited this dramatic display; we had been out in the open with him for 20 minutes before he reared. I was, however, pleased to be able to record this unique behavior and learn something new about this amazing species. It's still the only time that I've witnessed this reaction in all my years of walking with caribou.

Wolves have coevolved with caribou through successive Ice Ages, each species forcing the selection of their fastest offspring for survival. For most of the year, wolves follow migrating herds, sometimes for hundreds of miles; thus, the life cycles

Left: Wolves and caribou have coevolved in the boreal forest as predator and prey.

Right: Wherever their ranges overlap, like in Newfoundland, black bears will prey on caribou, especially during calving season.

of these two species are closely intertwined. Wolves suspend their nomadic ways only to den and raise pups that are soon strong enough to rendezvous with their tireless prey. Caribou herds can be hard to intercept in the immense landscape of the Far North. Driven by the need for fresh pasture and to escape biting flies, tundra caribou never stop traveling, and this makes it harder for predators to find them. Wolves can easily bring down healthy mature caribou but typically hunt the "rear guard," animals too weak or injured to keep up with the main body of the herd.

Grizzly and black bears prey on caribou where and when their ranges overlap, primarily taking advantage of calving season. In Finland, wolverines have become the primary predator of reindeer, killing three times more animals than wolves and bears combined.

An emerging trend, observed in Svalbard, Norway, has revealed that polar bears are regularly targeting caribou. Polar bears chase a caribou into the ocean, catch it, drown it and then haul it back to land to consume it. The predation of caribou

A grizzly bear runs across the tundra. When encountering caribou, bears will sometimes test them by quickly running at them, hoping to spot weakness or injury.

by polar bears, believed to be rare before 2000, is now on the rise due to the rapid disappearance of sea ice in the Far North. Polar bears have had to switch to more land-based prey and have adapted this highly specialized strategy for hunting caribou, passing on the technique to their cubs.

In the spring, caribou look the worse for wear. They are skinny from the hardships of winter and the travails of migration. Their dense winter pelage sheds in clumps, exposing the dark summer coat beneath and creating a ragged patchwork of fur. Males molt sooner than the maternal cows and yearlings, which likely protects the gestating females from the elements for a little while longer.

A wolverine feeding on a caribou carcass in the mountains of the Arctic National Wildlife Refuge in Alaska.
PHOTO CREDIT: PETER MATHER/ MINDEN PICTURES

Opposite: A grizzly bear roams the expansive foothills of the Alaska Range, always on the lookout for its next meal.

Migratory caribou herds are defined by their calving grounds. Like sea turtles and ocean salmon, caribou mothers return to the place where they were born to bring forth new life. In the spring, all of the maternal cows and their yearlings begin the journey back "home."

Caribou that migrate north of the Arctic Circle time their arrival at their calving grounds close to their collective due date. If they start their migration early, they can travel at a moderate pace. If the caribou leave late, they must move almost continuously to reach the calving grounds in time. Severe weather events may force herds to take lengthy detours, sometimes adding hundreds of kilometers to the migration route. Prolonged delays may result in calves being born on the trail, greatly increasing their mortality.

Timing is also critical because the earlier the maternal herd arrives, the more time the cows and yearlings have to build up their strength to withstand the impending onslaught of insects.

Although caribou can migrate in herds of tens of thousands of animals, when the maternal cows reach the calving grounds, the long, resolute lines of females and their yearlings disperse into smaller and smaller wandering groups. The pace slows, and the exhausted caribou fall into a relaxed rhythm of resting and grazing. By distributing themselves more evenly over the landscape, there is less chance of maternal cows attracting predators.

These ancient sanctuaries, relied on by caribou for millennia, are unique in that they provide the best conditions for the next generation to survive.

Birthing areas are typically more sheltered from storms. Calves can easily succumb to deadly combinations of freezing rain and high windchill. Strong winds can tumble young caribou and cause injury.

Long-established calving grounds experience an earlier melting of snow cover, which means that nutritious foods like grass shoots and protein-rich flower buds are available sooner. This new vegetation is essential for cows to regain their strength after the rigors

A polar bear in Svalbard, Norway, feeds on a reindeer which has drowned and been dragged to shore. Many believe that reindeer are a new, alternative food source for polar bears in response to lessening sea ice.

PHOTO CREDIT: JEANETTE FRASER

of migration and of lactation, which is biologically expensive. It is also critical for calves, which must store enough energy in their small bodies to meet the demands of the coming winter.

Lastly, birthing sites for tundra caribou are always wide-open spaces, where air circulates reliably to reduce insect harassment, and approaching predators can be spotted from a distance.

Caribou only deliver one calf per year because gestation consumes so much of a cow's energy stores. Their young come into the world without preamble. Labor can last minutes or up to an hour, and newborns have an average weight of 13 pounds. Cows will consume the placenta, so that the bloody afterbirth doesn't attract predators.

Just as quickly as they are born, the calves are on their feet and nursing, and in an hour or two they begin sampling the new green plants. Aside from the milk of

A caribou mother of the Porcupine herd, in the Arctic National Wildlife Refuge in Alaska, licking her newborn calf.

PHOTO CREDIT: PETER MATHER/ MINDEN PICTURES

marine mammals, caribou milk is the richest, being 20 percent fat, and youngsters can double their weight in two weeks.

The first few days of a calf's life are dedicated to establishing the maternal bond. It is critical that mother and newborn learn to recognize each other by smell and sound. For tundra caribou, imprinting is the only way the maternal pair can stay together in the confusion of the larger herd. From the moment it is born, the cow will frequently lick and nuzzle her calf, memorizing its scent. This intimate contact also passes on beneficial bacteria to colonize the infant's gut with the microflora critical for ruminants.

After the newborn is clean and fed, the mother will walk away and coax her calf, calling for it to follow. Caribou offspring are highly precocious, teetering after their mothers within hours of birth. A cow will lead her infant over surprisingly long distances in the first days of life to build up its strength, and soon they will join nursery groups of cows with similar-aged young. Chasing and playing with other calves further increases the youngster's agility and stamina. Survival depends on movement, and movement means keeping up with the constantly traveling bands.

A barren-ground caribou mother and calf crossing a river during migration in the Arctic National Wildlife Refuge in Alaska.
PHOTO CREDIT: INGO ARNDT/MINDEN PICTURES

To learn each other's voices, a female caribou will call out to her young whenever she moves on, and the calf will bleat in response. This vocalization is essential for reuniting the pair if they become separated. Stampedes ignited by predator attacks or insect panics often result in lost calves and frantic mothers. Natural elements like rushing rivers that lie across the migratory path can also divide the maternal pair. Caribou cows are extremely dedicated parents. Females call out and search tirelessly when their young go missing and are often rewarded for their persistence. When tragedy strikes, cows have been known to hover by their calf's body for days, even returning to the carcass after rejoining the herd.

Almost all calves of large tundra herds are born in the span of one week or less. This phenomenon, called synchronous birth, gives the newborns the advantage of safety in numbers. A predator scanning the herd for easy pickings would find it difficult to single out one animal in a cast of thousands. In addition, calves are

A growing calf nurses during late summer.

45

Opposite: In the first few days after birth, caribou cows and calves are very vocal, constantly calling to each other.

born with light brown fur, making them almost indistinguishable from the spring tundra. Yet in spite of these evolutionary advantages, caribou calf mortality is high. Up to 40 percent of young perish every year, either eaten, lost, starved or carried away in strong currents.

Calves experience the highest predator toll in their first two weeks of life. At this time, the tiny caribou are too slow and ungainly to outrun a bear or wolf. Their small size makes them targets for many carnivores, and not just apex predators. Golden eagles, foxes, wolverines and lynx also take many young. At 2 weeks old, calves are fast and agile enough to outrun a wolf, and as a consequence predation dramatically declines.

As spring progresses, caribou across North America enthusiastically transition to a diet of new willow leaves, sedges, flowering plants, mushrooms and other fresh

A calf comes to its mother's call.

46

A calf sleeps on the tundra.

growth. Cotton grass grows in abundance on the Arctic plains, and its buds are especially rich in proteins. Some speculate that the remarkable size of the tundra herds is directly related to the millions and millions of these plants that proliferate in the Arctic spring.

Hard on the heels of the tundra greening comes a proliferation of deadlier kind: parasitic insects. Warble flies lay their eggs on the tundra caribou's legs in the summer when the skin is relatively exposed. These parasites plague caribou like a sci-fi horror film, spending the winter migrating up beneath the animal's skin. In the spring, they erupt along their backs and hang swollen and visible where the thick fur has fallen away, ready to drop and complete their life cycle.

Another insect menace are the horrendous botflies that lay their living larvae in the caribou's nose. Migrating deep into the folds of the animal's sinuses, botfly larvae grow large enough to obstruct the host's air passages. Chronic coughing is an attempt by caribou to rid themselves of these parasitic masses.

On one of my tundra trips, I witnessed firsthand how terrified a caribou can become when hearing the nearby buzz of a botfly. I had found a mature bull standing by a small kettle pond. He was dozing, with his eyes closed for minutes at a time, swaying gently in the breeze. There was no real photo op, so I sat down on the nearby hillside and waited. Suddenly his eyes popped wide open and he bolted away at a dead run for 200 yards, did a 180 and came sprinting back, head tipped, nostrils flared, eyes wide open. He dashed past, coming within a few feet of me, and went up and over a nearby ridge, and I never saw him again. I hope that he outmaneuvered the pesky parasitic fly! Far more important that he get away than posing for a photo!

As the tundra warms up under the high sun, caribou dispel heat by panting and circulating air over their sparsely haired extremities and patches of bare skin. At the same time, stagnant pools of water become incubators for huge swarms of

A caribou mother keeps a watchful eye for predators.

A healthy female calf drinks rainwater from a puddle in the rocks.

mosquitoes, which relentlessly assail Arctic caribou. During the warmest weeks of the summer, caribou find a measure of relief from the fearsome swarms in a variety of ways. They will roam across the tundra, moving quickly into the wind to evade their buzzing attackers. They will climb up ridges to look for cooler, moving air. Caribou may crowd together on patches of remaining snow or plunge into lakes or the ocean.

At their peak, the infestations will drive the tundra caribou to concentrate in vast herds, numbering as many as fifty to one hundred thousand animals, all in continuous motion, all pressed together to expose the least amount of individual skin. These giant animal aggregations are known as "tandara." Among caribou, these throngs last only a few weeks until the weather cools and insects lessen. The release from this torment allows Arctic caribou to finally focus intensely on feeding in preparation for the next major migration, from tundra to taiga, which begins in mid-August.

Opposite: Caribou members of the Porcupine herd seek relief from biting insects in the Arctic National Wildlife Refuge in Alaska.
PHOTO CREDIT: MICHIO HOSHINO/ MINDEN PICTURES

CARIBOU FROM COAST TO COAST

ntercepting the fall caribou migration is a bucket list-worthy experience for any naturalist, biologist or wildlife photographer. It is a privilege to witness these iconic animals at their peak annual condition in the seemingly endless wild landscape that they inhabit. The first trip that I took with my son, Andrew, to the Far North turned out to be the right place at the right time. At 13, Andrew was big enough to maneuver the challenging landscape while searching for wildlife.

On this expedition, we had two magical days on the tundra with a bachelor group of barren-ground caribou that were slowly migrating to join the main herd for the autumn rut. Some ridges in the Far North have very little vegetation at their peak due to wind exposure. Many animals use these barren stretches as easy walking paths, which become smooth trails of packed rock for easier hiking.

A bachelor group of barren-ground caribou bulls, at various stages of velvet shedding, migrates toward their autumn rutting grounds.

A stunning specimen of a barren-ground caribou walks past Andrew and me in the high alpine setting. Freshly shed velvet still clings to part of his antler.

We'd traveled along the twisting and turning ridgetop, identifying tracks and droppings as we went. As we progressed, valleys revealed themselves on either side. After a few kilometers, we peered into a valley and spotted half a dozen caribou bulls feeding. Naturally, they saw us immediately, so we carefully moved 30 yards down from the ridgetop so we wouldn't stay silhouetted against the skyline, as we didn't want to intimidate the small herd.

After a brief wait and a slow approach, they accepted our presence, and we were delighted to photograph them and observe their pre-rut migration behavior. We spent the remainder of the day in their company, mimicking their pattern of wandering and resting. Come evening, we thanked them and retraced our footsteps back to the campsite.

As we set out in the predawn light the following morning, our sole ambition was to find the cooperative group again for another opportunity to document more of their behavior. We trekked back to the valley where we'd left them, but were disappointed to discover that it was now empty. Little did we know that the day ahead of us would offer one of our most memorable adventures.

With the valley devoid of caribou, we continued farther along the ridge path. Half an hour later, we sat down and studied the landscape with our binoculars. That's when Andrew spotted them — tiny, moving white dots of caribou nearing the top of a saddle between mountains a few kilometers away and about 4,000 feet above us. Wow! They'd really covered ground overnight! It was a relief to locate them, but they were a long way away.

We discussed our options for a few minutes and decided that since we'd already traveled so far to be in this magical place, we would go for it and try to catch up with them. At that moment, they didn't seem to be in a big hurry, and we hoped that they would stay near their current position for the couple of hours it would take us to reach them.

Part of the challenge of this hike was that we quickly lost sight of the caribou as we entered the valley below them. With no visual confirmation of their whereabouts as we hiked the thousands of feet of game trails toward the pass, we tried our best to remain motivated.

The bulls approach the mountain pass during fall migration.

A herd of woodland caribou on the move in the northern boreal forest.

Persistence paid off on this day. As we crested a rise near what we thought was the top, we spotted the small herd of bulls grazing a few hundred yards away.

Accurately assessing the effort required to reach a subject in the open country of the Far North can be a challenge. From where we'd spotted the bachelor herd, we thought that they were nearing the summit of the 1,500-meter mountain. Once we reached them, we realized this was not the case, as they were still about half a kilometer from the top.

There were tremendous specimens in this group, including what was probably the largest antlered bull that I've ever seen. We had about an hour with them during the late afternoon as we paralleled and filmed them as the caribou continued to climb.

Eventually they made it to the crest of the saddle and went over and out of sight. That was the last that we saw of this stunning group. They would soon join the much larger herd to the north and challenge one another for the right to pass on their genetic line.

Before beginning the long descent, Andrew and I relaxed on the tundra, marveling at the encounter that we'd just shared while taking in the spectacular view. We arrived back at camp as darkness fell, completing a near-perfect day on the land with these magnificent nomads.

All caribou and reindeer throughout the world are considered to be the same species (*Rangifer tarandus*), with many subspecies globally, the primary ones being: barren-ground caribou (*R.t. groenlandicus*); Dolphin and Union caribou (*R.t. groenlandicus x pearyi*); Grant's caribou (*R.t. granti*), which refers to the migratory herds of the continental northwest; woodland caribou (*R.t. caribou*); Peary caribou (*R.t. pearyi*); Svalbard reindeer (*R.t. platyrhynchus*); European reindeer (*R.t. tarandus*); Finnish forest reindeer (*R.t. fennicus*); and the Siberian tundra reindeer (*R.t. sibiricus*).

Within all of the subgroups, the caribou females are smaller than the males, from two-thirds to half the size. On average, mature bulls weigh 350 to 400 pounds. Cows make up for this size disparity in longevity, potentially living to a ripe old age of 15 years compared to 8 to 10 years, which is the average life span of healthy males.

Coat coloration varies among subspecies, and all caribou's fur changes with the seasons. Summer coats are short with fine hair, ranging from deep brown to slate grey with white trim. Males have a pale patch of hair called a mane around their necks, which grows thicker and longer for winter.

North American barren-ground caribou spend spring, summer and autumn migrating through the vast open tundra north of the Arctic Circle. They are the most abundant ecotype and travel the longest of any land animal between seasonal ranges. Barren-ground caribou are numerous for several reasons. This subspecies' range is so remote and the weather there so extreme that up until now, these two factors have largely protected the land and the caribou from human activity, leaving critical migration routes intact. The massive annual swarms of biting insects have also kept humans and most other animals out of the caribou's range. Some barren-ground habitat is provincially and/or federally protected, including sensitive

Caribou herd migrating across the tundra in the Arctic National Wildlife Refuge in Alaska. An incredible perspective to appreciate these time-worn trails. Will there be views like this a hundred years from now?
PHOTO CREDIT: MICHIO HOSHINO/ MINDEN PICTURES

A female caribou and a pair of playful calves from the herd wander the coast during autumn migration.

calving areas. Lastly, the sheer size of the barren-ground herds have allowed them to rebound more effectively when their population numbers are impacted by habitat degradation, overharvesting or disease.

The migration patterns and range of caribou are as varied as the herds themselves and have evolved to ensure the survival of the species in their unique environments. Caribou roam to both preserve and exploit the best habitat for each season and to source the most reliable food. They thrive in many different types of terrain and can be found from alpine meadows in the Rocky Mountains to the bogs of Newfoundland and on the most remote islands of the high Arctic.

The range of herds can be confined to a small ocean peninsula or encompass tens of thousands of square kilometers. Some caribou travel through snow for weeks to find safe birthing sites, and others swim to remote islands to ensure the survival of calves that would likely succumb to intense predation on the mainland. And certain Newfoundland herds have the luxury of being homebodies, calving close to or within their winter range. Overwintering in boreal or taiga forest habitats, where the protective timber keeps the snow loose, makes it easier for caribou to paw down to the food beneath.

The continuous movement of the largest herds in North America over a vast range is a strategy that usually protects any one area from being overbrowsed. The main dietary staple of any caribou is lichen, which is resilient but slow-growing. The animal's nomadic life cycles allow lichen at least a full year of recovery before the throng's return. I have spent many days watching caribou as they graze their way across the taiga and have observed that even when they encounter an especially rich patch of forage, they will grab a few mouthfuls and move on. It's almost as if their legs are in charge and they take what they can as the land passes beneath their feet.

Migration routes are flexible when necessary, diverging in response to weather influences. In spite of this, caribou frequently encounter hazardous conditions they cannot avoid, and injury and lameness are common. Caribou are always reluctant to cross water. It cuts off their avenues of escape and makes them vulnerable to attack by wolves lurking in the brush along the water's edge. Torrential rivers, swollen with spring runoff, can sweep away even the strongest swimmers, and if spring comes quickly, frozen rivers can break up without warning, releasing slabs of fast-moving ice that can crush traversing caribou.

Conservation of energy is a key component of long-distance caribou migration, and animals typically follow the path of least resistance, such as walking in single file or following the hard ground of frozen rivers and lakes or windblown ridges. In the communities of the Far North, it is not unusual to see groups of caribou availing themselves of human-made roads. The earlier the start of the spring migration, the greater chance that bodies of water encountered on the trails will be solidly frozen, greatly reducing the physical toll on the maternal herd, which is the first caribou group to leave the wintering range in the spring.

The longest land migration in the world is a drama that unfolds far from any audience, on nature's grandest and most austere stage. Few people actually witness the annual mass exodus of barren-ground caribou from their wintering sites in the boreal taiga to calving areas in the Arctic, but many know of their perilous treks over hundreds of kilometers of remote northern wilderness.

At some point in the endless winter routine of sniffing out food and cratering through the snow,

A barren-ground caribou herd, led by a mature cow, migrates single file across a snowy scene in Alaska, on their way to the spring calving grounds.
PHOTO CREDIT: MICHIO HOSHINO/ MINDEN PICTURES

The Porcupine caribou herd crossing the Blow River, Yukon, Canada. See if your eye can follow the trail of caribou off toward the horizon.

PHOTO CREDIT: PETER MATHER/ MINDEN PICTURES

a mature cow will find her muzzle lifted and pointing north, her furry hooves trotting along with new purpose and the sheltering taiga forests already a distant memory. A long line of pregnant females and their yearlings will form behind the leader, closely spaced along the trail she has broken through the snow, conserving precious energy for the weeks of travel ahead. Perhaps the weight of the unborn calves stirring in their bellies, the scents carried in the air or even the feel of the snow have set their feet into this resolute rhythm. Whatever the combination of factors, the urge to move as spring approaches is powerful and spurs the great maternal herd toward the northern horizon.

As calving season approaches, female barren-ground caribou begin moving toward the all-important birthing area on the Arctic coastal plains. For millennia, barren-ground caribou have journeyed across the land on ancient trails that cut deeply across the landscape, some as old as 27,000 years. They struggle across violently surging rivers, plod defiantly against fierce winds and blinding blizzards and endure intense en route predation by wolves and humans, all in an effort to bring the next generation of caribou into the world.

The movement of caribou to their calving grounds is led by older females. They take turns guiding the groups across the rugged land. Non-maternal cows and young males will leave later, and mature bulls will delay for two or three weeks before departing to rendezvous with the main herd on their summer range.

Cows can live up to 15 years in the wild; they are the knowledge keepers of the herd. They learn the migration route first in the footsteps of their mothers, following as young calves and again as yearlings. They continue their nomadic lives in the wake of experienced matriarchs that have survived the rigors of the trail and remember them best. The ancestral trails are the most reliable routes across the landscape, tried and tested by hundreds of generations of caribou. They lead to narrows and shallow spots that provide the best crossings over waterways and to mountain passes with the least amount of snowpack.

How caribou find their way back to a small area over vast distances is still not entirely understood. That they are excellent navigators is evidenced when certain conditions derail migration and force the animals to veer off course, sometimes for hundreds of kilometers, yet they still manage to reconnect to the ancient routes. Herds may choose to overwinter in nontraditional areas, but they always find their way unerringly back to the calving grounds.

The northernmost stretch of the western ranges of North America, one of the few intact wilderness systems on Earth, is annually crisscrossed by Canada's largest caribou population: the barren-ground Porcupine herd, which is 200,000 animals strong. Apart from the Dempster Highway that stretches between Dawson City and Inuvik, there is no other break in the wilderness as caribou move between winter and summer ranges. They roam an area of about 240,000 square kilometers between Alaska and westernmost Canada, but congregate en masse in the Arctic National Wildlife Refuge and the Yukon North Slope to give birth on the coastal

Aerial of the migrating Porcupine caribou herd crossing a river in the Arctic National Wildlife Refuge in Alaska.
PHOTO CREDIT: PETER MATHER/ MINDEN PICTURES

A woodland caribou appears from the conifer forest in Newfoundland, Canada.

plains of the Arctic Ocean. Although caribou can travel up to 80 kilometers a day, the tremendous northward movement of the maternal herd to the calving grounds still takes two months, crossing four mountain ranges, hundreds of passes and dozens of rivers.

After the majority of caribou females have given birth along the coastal plains and the newborns are up and running, the nursery herd, as well as the recently arrived non-maternal females and young males, waste no time swinging around to their post-calving summer range. At the first sign of mosquitoes, the caribou unite, absorbing the last groups of mature bulls by midsummer. The huge herds travel back east into the prevailing wind and will remain in aggregations throughout the fall breeding season. By the time the caribou return and disperse into their winter range, the land will be snow-covered and the pace of migration will slow into daily cycles of foraging and retreats into open areas, such as frozen lakes or meadows, for rest and rumination, while keeping an eye out for predators.

When the snow is light, caribou range widely in small bands. As the snow deepens in midwinter, they become more sedentary, concentrating in regions of food security. Migration for caribou never really stops, in the endless search for nourishment and avoidance of predators and seasonal insects.

Research on when caribou begin their spring marathon, and why, has recently been conducted using modern telemetry and GPS satellite tracking systems. New and old data collected from over 1,000 collared animals in a number of different caribou groups across 3,000 kilometers of the Arctic Circle has revealed a pattern of synchronized departure in migratory herds. Scientific evidence shows that caribou all across North America are triggered to start their spring migration not by day length or availability of vegetation, as was previously believed, but by large-scale, ocean-driven climate cycles, particularly the Pacific Decadal Oscillation, a climate pattern similar to El Niño or La Niña, but 20 to 30 years in duration. In response to these forces, caribou herds from Hudson Bay to northern Alaska begin their annual start toward their summer range within days of one another.

Researchers have also discovered that summer conditions play an important role in the duration of the following spring's migration. The arrival time at the calving grounds is important for the reproductive success of the herd. The earlier, the better, and the timing seems to be heavily dependent on the weather conditions of the summer before. During cooler summers, caribou expend less energy avoiding insects and more time eating. A stronger maternal population with enough individual fat reserves will cover distances more quickly and be less impacted by the

A woodland caribou stag crosses a waterway in remote Newfoundland, Canada.

A herd of woodland caribou traverse the rocky Newfoundland coastline.

Opposite: Tracks reveal that a herd of caribou recently traveled along this sandy cove.
PHOTO CREDIT: PILI PALM-LEIS

scarcities of the snow-covered migration route when they set out the following year.

Delays in migration can have a significant impact on calf mortality. In July, millions of mosquitoes and biting flies hatch on the marshy tundra. Cows arriving later to the calving grounds may find that the all-important bonding time with their newborns is disrupted by swarms of insects that can drain a quart of blood from a single caribou in one week. Caribou mothers, frantic to escape the biting bugs, may spend more time seeking relief than feeding and nursing. Calves can even be tormented to death by insects. The barren-ground caribou's resilience is extraordinary given the challenges that they encounter through the seasons.

A barren-ground caribou herd of personal interest, due to many close encounters with its members during photography expeditions, is the one that roams within the expansive 19,187-square-kilometer wilderness of Denali National Park and Preserve in Alaska. Here, caribou are constantly being researched, teaching us more about their natural history and the predator/prey relationship fluctuations in this large ecosystem. The Denali herd, which largely remains in the park, mostly on the north side of the Alaska Range, once numbered over 20,000 back in the 1930s. It reached its lowest numbers of about 1,000 animals in the 1970s, while harvesting was still permitted. Today's population is estimated to be just over 1,700 animals, and they have taught us a lot about caribou biology through observation while filming them.

The caribou of the Western Arctic herd, Alaska's largest, were the focus of a GPS-collar research project from 2010–18 to ascertain what triggers animals to begin their autumn migration. The results indicated that both falling temperatures and the arrival of snow were the catalysts that sparked the seasonal shift. However, if the animals encountered warming temperatures and a reduction in snow during their migration, they would delay and focus their energies back on foraging. When the temperatures dropped again and snow returned, they'd resume their trek to their wintering grounds. It's worthwhile to note that the study found that the autumn

migration commences later and later each year, and biologists believe that this trend will persist as global warming impacts the north.

The woodland caribou (also called boreal caribou)'s range differs from that of the barren-ground caribou, as it coincides with the mantle of boreal forest that spans the continent and the open taiga forests along the Hudson Bay coast.

Migratory diversity also occurs within the woodland groups themselves, with some individuals roaming and returning, and others staying put year-round. Woodland caribou females leave the group to calve in the most inaccessible parts of their range, often close to water, as it provides the best escape route for these strong swimmers.

Woodland caribou are now only found in northern Canada, from Newfoundland through to British Columbia and the southern Yukon. Historically, woodland caribou were found in every province, including the Maritimes, where the species was extirpated in the 1920s.

In the 1980s and 1990s, eastern migratory woodland caribou comprised the largest herd in the world. The 800,000 animals of the George River herd roamed over 100,000 square kilometers through Nunavut, northern Quebec and Labrador. They migrated thousands of kilometers between winter and calving ranges like their barren-ground cousins. Overbrowsing and the subsequent habitat degradation caused the population of this mega-herd to collapse. This decline was likely

Migration requires caribou to swim across many waterways, both rivers and lakes.

significantly aggravated by human activity. By 2010, the herd numbers had dropped to 74,000, then to 14,200 by 2014.

In 2020, the population census recorded only 8,100 caribou, less than one percent of the herd's historic number — but the good news is that it's up from 5,500 animals in 2018. At the current rate of decline and without serious limits on harvesting, the herd could be functionally extirpated in five years. When caribou populations experience catastrophic reductions, much of the herd memory is lost, and migration can unfortunately be permanently disrupted.

On the island of Newfoundland, the number of woodland caribou in the mid-90s was approximately 92,000. Today, the current population estimate is around one-third of that, or 30,000 animals, spread across 14 geographically identified herds.

The mountain caribou is an ecotype of the woodland caribou subspecies that roams the mountains of the continental northwest. They are the largest-bodied of the caribou ecotypes, with longer legs for plowing through deep winter snowpack. Sometimes called the "Grey Ghosts," their darker coloration allows them to blend into the dense forest habitat. The most extensive stretch of interior temperate

A sunset view of a caribou calf as it follows and learns from its mother on the tundra.

A trio of critically endangered mountain caribou in the Tonquin Valley, by the Ramparts mountain range, in Jasper National Park, Alberta, Canada.

PHOTO CREDIT: SIMONE HEINRICH

rainforest on Earth is found in the subranges of the Rockies in British Columbia. Within its dim green halls of towering trees, precarious numbers of elusive mountain caribou browse on arboreal lichens found nowhere else in the world. These ground, and hanging, lichens grow in abundance only in forests that are a century old or older.

The mountain caribou ecotype has evolved a unique life cycle, migrating seasonally between the dramatically different altitudes of their habitat. Of all mountain caribou, 98 percent live in British Columbia.

The south and central herds thrived in the previously undisturbed temperate rainforests of the province's interior. Small, scattered groups of mountain caribou follow a double migration pattern up and down between the lush lowland valleys and the high alpine barrens, calculated to access food while avoiding predators. Valleys as low as 460 meters above sea level exist in the subranges of the Rocky Mountains, thick with a dense mixture of rainforest and boreal forest. These shadowy stands of old-growth trees are often fringed by peaks as high as 3,600 meters. In the winter, high elevation forests collect an extraordinary amount of snowpack, often in excess of 10 feet. Mountain caribou, with their snowshoe-like hooves, spend late winters there, browsing on black-haired tree lichens that dangle from the top limbs of conifers that would be impossible to reach without the deep drifts. Some elevated alpine tundra slopes remain relatively snow-free due to high winds, and mountain caribou will also seek out these areas above the snowpack, cratering to expose ground lichens, safe from predators that keep to the shallow snow cover of the lowlands.

When the temperatures rise in the spring, mountain caribou descend to forage on fresh spring vegetation exposed by advanced snowmelt in the warmer valleys, spreading out through the shady forests in small groups to avoid detection by wolves and bears.

As the snow retreats up the mountains in later spring, the caribou return to the windy alpine barrens to escape biting insects and give birth in remote, inaccessible locations. The rest of the summer is spent feeding in wet subalpine forests and meadows. Fall sees the herds back in the valleys, browsing on small shrubs and windblown lichens, waiting for the snowpack to accumulate again at the high tree line. Mountain caribou migration patterns have evolved to take advantage of the distinct biomes in the Canadian Rockies.

Ninety-eight percent of the remaining mountain caribou that exist in Canada have herds confined to the northwest corner of the continent, with the majority of animals residing in southern Yukon. Until recently, the southern mountain and central mountain caribou units extended into Washington, Idaho and Montana, but the American populations are now extirpated. The mountain caribou ecotype is listed as an endangered subspecies by COSEWIC (Committee on the Status of Endangered Wildlife in Canada).

Peary caribou are the smallest of all the North American subspecies. They are more closely related to the Svalbard reindeer population, 400 miles north of Norway, than their larger cousins to the south. Females weigh an average of 130 pounds,

A member of the northern mountain caribou of the interior forests of central British Columbia emerges through the fog like a ghost. Let's hope that this subspecies doesn't become one.

PHOTO CREDIT: ERIC BREWER

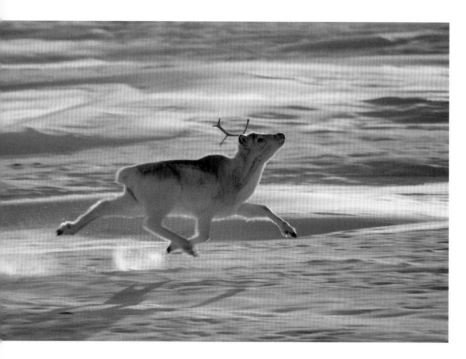

A Peary caribou running on Ellesmere Island, Nunavut, Canada.

PHOTO CREDIT: JIM BRANDENBURG/ MINDEN PICTURES

and males weigh almost double that. With a population of approximately 13,200 mature animals, they inhabit the high Arctic islands of Nunavut and the Northwest Territories. Peary caribou are mostly white in winter to blend into the snowscape and silvery with a dark grey or brown saddle in the summer.

River valley slopes and other moist environments, as well as upland plains with their abundant grasses, sedges and willows, provide the easiest access to summer plants for this subspecies. In the winter, Peary caribou forage on exposed hilltops and beach ridges where the winds scour snow down to a thinner layer. In the spring, the intense sun sometimes melts the surface snow, which percolates down and refreezes in thick layers, making it impossible for Peary caribou to break through and reach the low-growing plants that they need. Necessity then forces these diminutive caribou to migrate great distances across the sea ice to other islands with more favorable snow conditions and available food. Using their superb orientation instincts, Peary caribou can travel up to 50 miles or more across shifting sea ice to reach a neighboring land mass.

Warmer summers due to climate change have temporarily benefited the Peary caribou herds, leaving more forage exposed for longer periods of the year. But with temperatures in the Arctic continuing to rise at three times the global average, the winter sea ice between the high Arctic islands may disappear, leaving the Peary caribou little choice but to stay put. As a result, they could overgraze their food supply or attempt to swim the distances they formerly traversed on ice. Lengthy water crossings in the Arctic Ocean would be perilous for this small caribou and leave them vulnerable to freezing, exhaustion or apex predators.

Caribou share their range with many other species, most of which they can swiftly outrun. In the continual effort to conserve energy, caribou will only flee a predator if directly attacked; otherwise, they just keep an eye on any animals entering the landscape.

There have been rare instances when I've taken images showing both caribou and moose sharing the same habitat. The first time it happened, four years ago, I was photographing a group of 10 woodland caribou in a grove in the boreal forest in Newfoundland. The caribou bull was feeding on his own in a small clearing when a movement caught my eye at the nearby tree line.

A closer look had me both confused and excited to see that a cow moose was entering the clearing and was heading directly toward the caribou! This was during the moose rut, so I was torn between taking photos or just watching what was about to unfold, as I'd never personally experienced these two species in such close proximity before.

The bull continued grazing, and as the cow moose approached, I snapped a few photos, waiting for him to lift his head to look toward the towering newcomer. He didn't! He just kept on eating as she walked by — a mere 20 yards away! I was surprised at how relaxed they were with each other. In hindsight, I realized that caribou and moose often intermingle on this big island and forage in much of the same habitat. I should've known that they'd be familiar with each other. It was an amazing moment to witness firsthand!

A rare photo from Newfoundland, Canada, illustrates the overlap of ranges between moose and caribou in the northern boreal forest.

THE ROLE
OF ANTLERS

A photo I took that best illustrates the rare, time-sensitive behavior of antler velvet shedding was captured on my first trek into caribou country. My brother Darren and I were camping in remote central Alaska and had received a great tip from a fellow photographer. He'd filmed three mature barren-ground caribou bulls earlier that morning, up a ridge about a mile away.

Darren and I eagerly headed in that direction and soon spotted them bedded up on a ridgetop, their tall antlers revealing their location.

The weather was changeable that day along the north side of the Alaska Range. Brilliant beams of light would break through the cloud cover, only to be snuffed out by duller, heavier overcast, with intermittent rain for good measure. The light wasn't great when we arrived, so we sat down on the soft alpine tundra and took in the magnificent scene in the company of these fine bulls.

A mature woodland caribou bull patiently spars with a feisty adolescent during the pre-rut.

The stunning heart-shaped antler formation on the bull shedding his velvet, where the strands hang like dreadlocks.

Opposite: To visually illustrate the differences in size and shape of the antlered mammals of North America, we've included a photograph of each species (moose, elk, mule deer and white-tailed deer), so that you can see the differences as well as appreciate the elaborate structure of caribou antlers.

After a while, they stood up and began to feed. One of them had antlers still fully clothed in velvet, another had stripped the fuzzy outer layer from his rack and the third was in the midst of shedding his — and looked like he was sporting some serious dreadlocks!

Removing the velvet, which supplies blood and nourishment to the rapidly growing bone from spring through summer, takes place once the antlers have completely hardened in early autumn. Bulls rub their rack against willow shrubs to peel off and discard most of this superfluous layer within a day or so.

The large, hanging strands can impede the animal's ability to see. Anything that blocks their view is intolerable to prey species, and they take pains to remove these blinders as quickly as they can.

The scent of this process can attract predators, such as wolves, as they have been known to wait for the protein-rich velvet snack to be left behind by the healthy caribou. That is, if the caribou doesn't eat it themselves for nourishment.

The velvet-shedding stage of the annual antler cycle happens in what seems like a blink of an eye. That's what made this timely encounter very special. Within a day or two of completing this painless process, the bull's rack will be washed clean from the morning dew, on shrubs as he rubs them or by the rain. The red color on the antlers is very fleeting and quickly becomes brown.

To document such an important biological behavior on my first trip to the northern taiga forest was like winning the lottery. The light turned out to be perfect as the caribou browsed their way across the ridge. The alternating cloud and sunshine was ideal for highlighting the vibrant autumn foliage, as well as this bull's crimson-colored rack. Shafts of light would pierce through the heavy sky and

Now that's a back scratcher! A tremendous rack does have its advantages.

Opposite: An image to highlight the size difference in male and female caribou antlers. Bulls remove their velvet in early September, and cows do so in early October.

illuminate the animals or part of the landscape for a dramatic effect. To top it all off, this striking animal's rack was in the shape of a heart when looking straight at the camera — picture-perfect!

The noble family of *Cervidae* is the phylogenetic home of North America's antlered mammals. It includes heavy hitters like moose, whose wide, palmated rack can span a staggering 6 feet and weigh up to 70 pounds; elk, with back-arching antlers so long they can scratch their own rumps by looking up; and impressive lightweights such as mule deer and white-tailed deer. Caribou antlers are a unique

A mature female caribou still in velvet, alert on the barrens.

Opposite, top: A pair of caribou cows rest along the northern coastline.

Opposite, bottom: Cow caribou spar, using their antlers to joust, establishing a dominance hierarchy.

hybrid: sturdy, semi-circular beams that in males often open into upper palms fringed with sharp tines. Caribou antlers are a marvel of evolution, and it's remarkable how varied these jousting crowns are among the cervid family.

"Double-shovel," "bez," "double back scratchers," "palmated forward-sweeping uppers" — these terms seem like the names of advanced snowboarding stunts. In fact, they all refer to the elaborate antler structures grown and shed annually from the heads of caribou.

Antlers have enthralled people since the dawn of time. These elaborate crowns of bone emerge annually from the heads of mostly male members of the deer family. Caribou are the exception, being the only species where both sexes annually grow antlers. The antlers grown by female caribou are smaller and more irregular than the male caribou, but serve several important functions.

Why are cow caribou the only members of the deer family to consistently grow antlers? The most accepted scientific hypothesis is that their primary purpose is to bestow a feeding advantage upon gestating cows during the harsh, long winter. Mature male caribou typically drop their antlers first, triggered by plummeting testosterone levels due to their rutting efforts and successes, effectively relieving themselves of a great deal of weight before the worst weather hits. Females keep their much lighter antlers until their calves are born in the spring. Biologists believe that this significant delay in antler shedding helps maternal cows defend the craters that they dig in the snow from other caribou, especially the much larger males. By keeping their antlers, the females become the dominant gender throughout the long winter months. By prioritizing the efforts of the pregnant

A female caribou rubs her antlers on a conifer shrub. Cows do this to strip the velvet from their rack in early October. As the month progresses, they may do it to get the attention of the dominant bull — it's one way of signaling that they're going into heat.

females when food resources are at their lowest, it best insures the survival of the female, the unborn young and, in turn, the species.

Female caribou also make use of their spiked headgear to spar with one another to establish a dominance hierarchy. This is applicable at any time of the year when they're wearing antlers, but is especially true during the rut, when more than one female can enter estrus at the same time. The dominant female will insist on receiving the herd bull's attentions before other cows that are in heat at the same time.

In autumn, female caribou also rub shrubs with their antlers, usually where the bull has already left his scent mark. This serves to draw the attention of the herd bull that the female is entering estrus and seeking his attention.

It's an astonishing fact that each caribou crown is unique to its bearer; no two animals grow the same rack. Antler size and shape are dictated by the animal's age, genetics, nutrition and overall health.

Mature male caribou sport the shovel or brow tine (or palm) that sprouts forward near the base (pedicel) of the antler that extends over the nose to guard the face and eyes during bouts of sparring and fighting that occur from September through the October rut. Each stag has a unique brow palm; most are a vertical blade of bone that has a varying number of small forward-pointing spikes at the front. The healthiest and genetically superior bulls sprout shovels from the base of both antlers, creating impressive double-shovel configurations over their nose.

Two barren-ground caribou, antlers fully grown but still sheathed in velvet, pose in unison on the early autumn tundra.
PHOTO CREDIT: ANDREW RAYCROFT

The second branch emerging from the main beam, a few inches above the brow palm, is called the bez. Bez typically grow from both antlers and in mature males form a multi-tined, palmated branch that curves forward above the bull's ears.

Almost halfway up each curving main beam, some bulls also grow a small rear-facing point that is commonly referred to as a "back scratcher."

As the main beam continues to curve back and up, it forms a forward-facing C shape and typically becomes thicker at the top, with additional tines that point skyward. A healthy, prime-aged bull can have antlers that exceed 50 inches (1.25 meters) in length.

The antler cycle begins each spring, triggered by increasing day length or photoperiod. Budding antlers emerge from the pedicel on the skull, covered in a soft, densely vascularized skin called "velvet." This encases the expanding antlers, grows

Opposite: The brow tine or shovel, the bez, back scratchers and multi-tined uppers are clearly visible on the antlers of this mature barren-ground caribou.

A pair of woodland caribou bulls cross a bog in Newfoundland. The velvet on their antlers is almost ready to peel away to reveal their new crowns of bone.

A pair of majestic barren-ground bulls cross a colorful ridgeline. One is still in velvet, while the other has stripped its rack free of its outer layer.

PHOTO CREDIT: ANDREW RAYCROFT

Right: A close-up of a caribou calf showing its antler growth at the end of its first summer.

Opposite: The antlers of a mature caribou bull can grow as much as 2.5 inches per day during early summer! This bull's rack is fully formed, and the first hint of velvet peeling has begun.

84

with them and supplies the necessary blood flow and nutrients to generate strong bone density over the months ahead. Males begin their antler growth in March, and cows in June.

Caribou antlers can grow up to an eye-popping 2.5 inches per day! Antlers are the fastest-growing bone on the planet.

This tremendous growth rate can't be sustained by nutrition alone. Mature males borrow calcium from their skeletal structure to fulfill this demand. This is replenished through diet once their antlers have finished forming and ossification is complete, typically before the physical demands of the rut.

By late July, a caribou's rack will be fully grown. The blood-engorged tissue will dry out but continue to cover the solid bone over the next month.

In the late summer, the decreasing day length triggers a hormonal response in males, releasing testosterone in a bull's system. Males begin stripping the velvet from their now fully hardened antlers. Males peel off their velvet from late August through early September, but females don't expose their antlers until early October.

A yearling male, called a "pricket" due to its velvet-covered, spiked antlers, is pictured with a mature woodland caribou bull.

Calves begin budding tiny velvet-covered antlers one month after birth. By autumn, male caribou calves can have noticeable thumb-sized prongs, which remain covered in velvet.

An interesting note: in Newfoundland, a male caribou in its second year is called a "pricket." Named after the spike on which a candle is stuck, the small, straight, unbranched antlers of these young males have inspired the name.

Why do a male's antlers grow larger as they enter their prime? For the first few years, a male caribou must devote the majority of his energy toward growing his body. A large, healthy male can eventually tip the scales at 400 pounds. Once his body has reached its peak potential around 4 years of age, more energy is invested into headgear to better compete with other males for the right to breed.

A pair of mature, northern barren-ground caribou bulls put their antlers to use shortly after velvet shedding.
PHOTO CREDIT: ANDREW RAYCROFT

I've had the rare opportunity to photograph the same bull over a few years. These images, taken two years apart (in 2019 and in 2021), illustrate how antlers grow from adolescence through to maturity. In the intervening time, this male woodland caribou grew considerably! Notice the similarities in the overall structure of his rack and how the antlers have become heavier with maturity, adding more elaborate points.

A bull is in his prime from 5 to 7 years old. Then, if he's fortunate enough to survive the trials of the rut, predators and winter past his 8th year, his health and stamina will gradually diminish, and his antlers will reflect his decline by becoming slightly smaller each consecutive year.

The primary function of antlers is to establish a dominance hierarchy. This is true for both sexes, but especially so for the males during the autumn rut. Bulls will spar dozens of times with other males in training for the upcoming battles of the rut, but also to establish their status and reduce the number of more dangerous fights during the energetic demands of the upcoming mating season. This hierarchy was obvious to us during our recent month spent in the company of woodland caribou. With these smaller bands, most bulls knew where they fit into the pecking order before the rut and rarely challenged others for a fight once the breeding harems began to form.

A mature woodland caribou bull makes a rub by thrashing his antlers on an evergreen shrub.

Are antlers meant to be embellished with evergreen sprigs for added attraction? This autumn, while photographing the wildlife in Newfoundland, we watched as a magnificent woodland caribou stag rubbed and thrashed his rack of antlers on a conifer bush. He worked at it for two solid minutes, which wasn't unusual; what was unusual — and made for a good chuckle and quick action of the shutter release — was that when he finally raised his head, a chunk of evergreen needles remained lodged in his brow tines, looking like an extravagant toupee.

Not to anthropomorphize, but he did seem proud of it for the several minutes he spent parading through his harem of females. To back up this notion, after he stopped walking, he gave his head a quick flick, and the branch easily sprang free and fell to the ground. Why didn't he do that right away? We'll never know, but the memory still brings a smile to my face.

He wore a very stylish hat when he finished rubbing! I don't believe that this was a planned headdress, but he didn't seem to mind, as he paraded around in front of the female for a few minutes before flicking it off!

Opposite: As a young bull feeds on the tundra, he approaches an antler shed from the previous year.

Left: Mark with a cool discovery from a day spent hiking in the Far North.

The annual antler cycle concludes with an impressive shed on the tundra. Notice the chew marks along the top — likely from a porcupine gnawing on the calcium-rich bone.

THE RUT

Each autumn, a spectacular event unfolds as the next generation of caribou are conceived across the vast northern barrens and boreal wilderness. This fall, for the first time, Pili and I remained in the company of caribou to witness the behavioral transitions spanning the entire rut. We watched and learned as the herds transitioned from the early pre-rut posturing of contending bulls, to the energetic ramp up as mating reached its peak during the rut, to the rest and recovery mode of the post-rut.

Observing caribou behavior over that month revealed many subtleties of their breeding season rituals. The surge of testosterone in the adult males manifested itself in swift mood changes from tolerance to aggression to affection, and sometimes we witnessed humorous interactions between a receptive female and her chosen suitor.

Preparation for the exertions of the rut begins in summer as mature bulls increase their weight by 20 percent or more between July and late September. They add

A mature woodland caribou bull scents the air
as he approaches a female during the autumn rut.

Left: A hefty woodland caribou bull, an excellent representation of his subspecies.

Right: A superb example of a barren-ground caribou bull in its prime during the September pre-rut.

Opposite, top: Male caribou spar with their antlers, training for the upcoming rut.

Opposite, bottom: A large barren-ground bull rubs a willow shrub during the pre-rut. Antler size, body mass and fighting technique will all be critical when it comes time to battle.

PHOTO CREDIT: ANDREW RAYCROFT

up to 3 inches of fat on their backs and rumps to meet the energetic demands of the rut. In addition to putting on the pounds, they also grow a thick mane, and their necks begin to swell significantly in September — doubling in girth by the time the rut starts. In early fall, a mature caribou bull is a sight to behold! With their glowing white mane contrasting against their sleek dark brown coat, their towering crown of antlers and their muscle mass and strength at their annual peak, caribou bulls are a regal portrayal of the power and fitness required to survive and procreate in the Far North.

Casual sparring bouts between males occur frequently throughout September. These friendly, tine-tickling contests serve to test out their newly hardened headgear and to build strength and technique for the far more serious battles that are sure to ensue during the October rut.

Bulls also use their hardened crowns to thrash both willow shrubbery and low-lying evergreens. With serious focus, mature males will rub or thrash a shrub for a couple of minutes, frequently pausing to assess their workmanship and decide if the rub has had enough scent deposited onto it. The bark on a section of the woody stem is rubbed off, sometimes as much as 2 feet of it, as the bull scent-marks his

Caption this expression! Call it friskiness, or call it something else — a caribou calf mounts a large bull, much to his surprise!

territory. Caribou researchers believe that this rubbing and thrashing behavior functions more as a male-to-female communication tool than as a threat to other males. The purpose could be to prime females that are approaching estrus.

Male caribou are capable of breeding at 1.5 years of age, but being capable and succeeding are two very different things. Yearling males are way too small in body and antler to contest for breeding rights, unless they find themselves in a dire situation where there are no adult males. It's not until bulls are at least 4 years old that they become active breeders, when both their body mass and antler size have grown large enough to challenge for dominance.

Body size also factors into a male's breeding success. It's not just about the antlers, but also the animal's physical strength and ability to win battles to gain the right to breed. Some researchers believe, after years of observing ungulates during the heated rut, that some successful males develop a strategy for fighting — such as picking the higher ground before engaging for added leverage.

Caribou are polygamous, where the barren-ground subspecies forms loose-tended groups of females, and woodland caribou often form harems. A dominant woodland bull has the stamina to defend a harem of about 10 females with calves.

Throughout the mating season, the herd bulls allow the male calves and even some male yearlings to stay in the group with the cows. It's something to witness the mature bull's aggression toward other adult males and then contrast that with their gentle tolerance shown toward the herd youngsters. On more than one occasion, we've watched as a male calf playfully rubs his velvet antler nubs against the giant rack of the herd bull. After a few seconds of indulgence, the bull typically responds with a gentle flick, and the calf goes on its way.

On another humorous occasion, we witnessed a male calf, likely inspired by the energies of the rut, try to mount the herd bull. The big bull, which was probably about eight times the size of the juvenile, glanced over his shoulder in what seemed like disbelief while turning and shaking off the youngster. Again, he responded with surprising gentleness given his current levels of testosterone and confrontational

A playful caribou calf rubs its fuzzy antler nubs against the rack a mature male.

attitude toward adolescent and older males. They're definitely not shown the same patience.

Herd bulls are very vocal during the rut, frequently bellowing out their guttural call to warn rival males to steer clear.

When another mature bull arrives on the scene, some of the females may trot over to check him out. If he's a contender and is willing to challenge for the right to breed, he will approach the harem or mating pair. Rival males will eye one another to assess their competition. This posturing is often enough to convince one of them to back down and retreat. If not, and if they're close in size, an intense fight will occur. Ears flattened and hackles raised, the bulls will walk close to one another in a parallel gait as they assess and try to intimidate their opponent, all the while displaying aggression. Once they're a few feet apart, they'll tip their towering antlers forward, smashing their tops together with impressive force. With hooves digging into the muskeg and debris flying, the intense twisting, turning and shoving may

Opposite: A bull caribou charges toward a satellite male to drive him away from his females.

A dominant woodland caribou bull chases a female to bring her back to his harem.

Opposite, top: Battle ensues
for the right to breed!

Opposite, bottom: The mature bulls
shove, twist and turn with fierce intensity!
Only the winner will have the right
to breed the nearby females. Much is
on the line.

A challenger arrives on the scene.

only last seconds, or it might continue for several minutes. Each bull will try to throw its opponent off-balance or, through brute power, force them to slip and fall, securing the upper hand. Both animals extend all effort in and focus on these strenuous bouts, which often leave both contestants temporarily exhausted.

The longer these fierce confrontations last, the greater the chance of injury or, in rare instances, even death. The pointed tines of their crowns can easily puncture or gore their opponent. They can tear a muscle or break ribs, which would effectively take them out of the game for the remainder of the rut. Such injuries put them at greater risk of predation, especially if they don't heal before the fast-approaching winter.

Witnessing the display of raw power while hearing the surprisingly loud antler clatter of a battle between two northern gladiators is an unforgettable display of strength and stamina that has been unfolding each autumn across the Far North for millennia. Fights usually end when one of the bulls recognizes defeat and quickly turns to flee while trying to evade the victor's punishing rack.

A mature cow urinates along the northern coastline. This behavior is bound to get the attention of the nearby bull to investigate whether or not she's entering estrus.

By spending several weeks in the taiga forests and adjacent tundra with various groups of woodland caribou, we noticed nuances in their behavior that we had overlooked during shorter trips. We realized that when female caribou entered estrus, it was a very gradual affair, a transition that I had previously assumed happened within a couple of days. Cows remain in peak breeding estrus for about 48 hours, when they'll mate several times with the dominant or herd bull. But the lead-up to the actual mating event is far more gradual and, at times, quite tender.

We noticed that when a female goes into heat, her interest in the male develops gradually, over many days. As her hormones increase and when she's about four or five days from being ready to breed, she will start to direct her attention to the dominant bull. Physically interacting with him more and more each day, she'll follow him closely, initiating courtship by nudging him with her head and antlers. Sometimes she'll rub her antlers against his in a mock spar when he's feeding, and

if he's still not returning her attentions, she may become bolder and gently poke his more sensitive areas with her headgear — which always elicits a response. Even in these situations, the bull responds with a relatively gentle rebuke.

As the cow becomes closer to the peak of estrus, the pheromones in her urine will change. This shift is smelled by the bull, and he'll do what's called a "flehmen response," or "lip curl." All members of the deer family practice this behavior, as the males have evolved a special organ in their upper oral region for this purpose.

A mature bull curls his lips (also known as a "flehmen response") to test if a nearby female is ready to breed.

The vomeronasal or Jacobson's organ tests the female's urine for sexual pheromones, revealing whether or not she's in full heat. As a bull approaches the spot where a cow has recently urinated, he'll pause to taste her urine. Lifting his head, with his upper lip curled back, the bull will inhale deeply for several seconds to confirm whether or not she is physically ready to mate.

It's interesting to note that caribou bulls don't lift their heads as much as their moose, elk and deer cousins, who stretch up higher and tip their heads back. Caribou extend their head forward and hold it lower when flehming.

By the fourth or fifth day of increased affection toward her chosen suitor, the cow will be at the peak of her estrus cycle and ready to successfully mate. Yes, it's the female that chooses the male — assuming that there's more than one mature bull to select from. At this point she will have the full and relatively non-stop attention of the bull. They will remain close to each other with prolonged physical contact, walking, feeding and resting together for the next couple of days. When the mating pair are standing together, and the bull isn't busy chasing off a contender, he will remain by her side or rear flank, waiting for the right time to attempt a mount.

Cows that aren't in heat remain with the band and carry on with their daily routine of feeding and resting, and chewing their cud, until their hormones spike and it becomes their turn to enter the breeding cycle.

When a bull isn't tending a cow that's in heat, he'll pace among the females in search of his next mate. Head bent low, he'll approach a female by driving his front hooves forcefully into the ground while licking his nose and lips, making a slurping sound as he nears the cow's hindquarters. The females are used to this

The bull will stay very close to the female that he's courting as long as she remains receptive.

Top: A mating pair of woodland caribou feeding in close proximity.

106

demonstration, and if they're not yet in heat, they'll respond by raising and bobbing their head in complaint and then trotting a few steps away — sending a clear message to the amorous male that they're not interested. The herd bull will go from cow to cow in hopes that one will respond favorably. If a cow is in heat, she will stand still and permit the bull to sniff her rear end.

As bands pass one another, they mix and mingle, creating a flurry of activity as the males size up one another, displaying, grunting and potentially battling for the females. The cows will often stay with and join the group with the more dominant male.

A harem of woodland caribou don't remain static in one location; they can travel several kilometers a day — following the lead cow, feeding, interacting and breeding — throughout their late-autumn range. The barren-ground subspecies doesn't form harems the same way their woodland cousins do. Their rut unfolds as the congregation migrates closer and closer to their winter range.

Most females become sexually mature at 3 years of age, with up to 25 percent of cows reaching breeding maturity during their second year. Eighty to ninety

Pacing through the nearby females, the bull scents the air as he searches for another cow that may be approaching estrus.

Two bands of caribou meet up along the northern coast. A competition for the females is a bound to ensue.

percent of the mature cows are successfully impregnated during the October rut. The majority of breeding occurs during the third week of the month. Historically, winter is knocking at the door, freezing up the landscape by this time across caribou country. This year, there was barely a flurry of snow during October, but we did have several heavy frosts to liven up the landscape.

After decades of photographing caribou, I was able to document caribou in the "act" of mating in 2021. The bull will usually make several unsuccessful attempts to mount, as the female often moves out of position during the first few tries. Once the bull manages to rise up onto the much smaller cow's back, copulation only takes a couple of seconds. One bull has the potential to breed with as many as 30 cows during the weeks of the autumn rut.

A harem of woodland caribou continue to move throughout their range during the rut.

110

Since there are more females than males in a herd, there is usually more than one female in heat at a time. When this happens, it's the dominant cow that will get to select her mate first. Other cows will either have to accept another male or, if in a harem, hope to garner the herd bull's affection at some point.

During the peak of the rut, dominant males eat less and undergo tremendous physical exertion in defending their females from other would-be suitors. Subordinate bulls are frequently and repeatedly charged and chased off with surprising speed and determination. This results in up to a 25 percent loss in body weight and can use up all of their fat stores, leaving them vulnerable as the season of scarcity sets in.

By the end of the rut, the mature bulls are spent, and adolescent males have an improved chance of breeding with any remaining females that go into heat near the season's end.

These subadults or satellite bulls sneak around the harem in hopes of breeding with a receptive female when the male isn't paying attention, or when he's preoccupied with another cow.

The act of mating is brief and only takes a few seconds.

This past October, we watched as one of the younger bulls, a persistent 3-year-old male, managed to separate one of the cows from the harem. With what appeared to be tremendous excitement, he chased and ran with her for hundreds of yards. Looping this way and that, they arced across the barrens. This female wasn't in heat at the moment, which is likely why the herd bull didn't give chase — or perhaps he was simply too tired at that late stage of the rut. However, she clearly wanted nothing to do with this up-and-comer.

As the young bull chased the female, he kept trying to jab her with his antlers, but she never stopped running. Eventually they circled back into the mix of the harem. The overzealous teenager had to stop short due to the presence of the mature bull. This example illustrates the control females have in the mating process, and despite being separated and chased for a bit by the young male, this experienced cow knew what she was doing and ended the brief escapade before anything more developed.

The main reason for early bull mortality is the toll that the rut takes on males of breeding age. By the time winter closes in, mature bulls have lost all of their

The dominant bull defends his females by chasing off all potential rivals.

fat reserves attempting to impregnate as many cows as possible. Many are injured from the violent battles that occur between rivals. Oftentimes, the cost paid by dominant bulls is a premature death.

Another benefit of spending the month with caribou was bearing witness to the shift in behaviors from the rut to post-rut. The rut had been in full swing, and now it seemed to be winding down surprisingly quickly. Evidence of this was the fact that the orbit of other bulls around the main herd began to shrink, and within days the ostracized males were permitted to rejoin. There didn't seem to be any more females in heat, as none of them were paying the dominant bull any mind. It was amusing to see that although the antagonism between the males was played out, they still bedded as far apart from one another as possible while still remaining with the group, even facing in opposite directions to ruminate. Eventually the herd bull relaxed, and even began to participate in relatively friendly sparring matches with the other males.

The adolescent male manages to separate a mature female from the herd and excitedly pursues her on the barrens.

As the rut concludes, other males are permitted to rejoin the group, but they're clearly not excited about one another's company at first. Notice the bedded positions of these two mature bulls.

As the rut concludes, and the bitter shift to winter is on the doorstep, barren-ground caribou complete their migration back to the taiga forests, and woodland caribou retreat to the boreal woods to shelter from the fierce, biting winds that will have returned. At this point, there is no longer any rivalry between the bulls, and they separate into bachelor groups. To conserve energy, the largest males shed their hefty antlered crowns in a matter of weeks. Cows and calves form their own collective and will live separately from the adult males until next year.

The timing of the rut has evolved to ensure that the next generation of caribou is born during the narrow window of ideal time during spring, after 230 days of gestation, when the frigid northern winter has retreated.

Opposite: A pair of impressive woodland caribou bulls feed in close proximity after the rut. They once again tolerate each other's company.

The rut is a challenging and exhausting affair! Bulls must rest and recovery quickly, as winter will arrive any day.

CONSERVATION AND THE FUTURE

Caribou and reindeer play a key role in Arctic ecosystems and provide irreplaceable socioeconomic value to many northern peoples. Across the circumpolar regions, *Rangifer tarandus* is the most abundant large terrestrial herbivore and is critical to northern ecosystems through its grazing and fertilizing effects on vegetation and by supporting predator populations. For Indigenous communities across the northern hemisphere, caribou and reindeer are the main component of subsistence hunting.

There have always been natural fluctuations in caribou and reindeer populations, some of them significant. During a particularly cold winter in the 1980s, coyotes crossed an ice bridge from Cape Breton to the island of Newfoundland, and the resident woodland caribou population plummeted as these new predators expanded

A sign cautions drivers to watch for caribou up the Maligne Canyon in Jasper National Park, Alberta, Canada. This mountain woodland caribou population is now extirpated, and like the caribou, this sign in no longer there.

A caribou herd rests on the barrens as the sun sets on another day in their homeland.

Right: An aerial photograph highlighting the rugged splendor of caribou country in Newfoundland, Canada, taken during one of our fly-in assignments.

120

their hunting grounds. Today, hunting has been limited to help the caribou recover, and the numbers of animals appear to have stabilized.

Conservation scientists and northern Indigenous peoples are deeply concerned by the recent rate and extent of caribou and reindeer decline across the planet. Research evidence indicates that a number of destructive factors are combining together for these animals and threaten the viability of this iconic Arctic species.

In the last 150 years, caribou have lost half of their historic range, and what is left continues to be fragmented and degraded by extractive industries, oil and gas projects,

Calf survival has plummeted in Newfoundland since the arrival of coyotes from across the ice bridge connecting to the mainland in the mid-1980s. This one is now easily large enough to outrun the wily canids.

Caribou populations are struggling in many parts of their range.

pollution and natural disasters, intensified by human-induced climate change. The devastating impact of these factors on caribou and reindeer numbers has made traditional levels of most subsistence hunting unsustainable. Many harvesting reductions and outright bans have been levied by the government or voluntarily adopted by First Nations communities, and the creation of management plans have bolstered waning caribou numbers.

In central Alaska, the successful recovery of the Fortymile herd of caribou is compelling evidence that a good management plan can boost the resiliency of even greatly reduced herds. From the population's peak in 1920 of over 500,000 animals, the herd crashed by 99 percent, with only 5,700 left in the 1970s. As a

Yes, there are actually road signs for caribou crossing in the Far North.

A caribou traveling along a northern roadway.

result of the voluntary suspension of hunting by Indigenous communities and years of conservation, the Fortymile barren-ground caribou herd has rebounded to 84,000 animals. There is now a brand-new harvest management plan to reintroduce subsistence hunting and keep the herd from overbrowsing their habitat.

As of the last census, the continent's last great caribou population, the Porcupine herd, is in good shape, with its numbers hovering around 200,000. The current American administration upheld the integrity of the Arctic National Wildlife Refuge and suspended development in the area, thereby protecting the Porcupine herd's critical calving grounds. The fate of this remarkable herd may depend upon future political decisions made far away from its magnificent range.

The future of other caribou and reindeer herds is not as promising.

Wild European reindeer survive now only in two countries. In the southern mountains of Norway, there are about 30,000–35,000 animals remaining, with the largest herd numbering 10,000. Of the rare Finnish forest reindeer, only 2,000 animals are left. They are confined to the small remaining tracts of boreal forest and are seldom seen by humans.

The remaining wild reindeer herds in Russia, formerly the world's largest populations, are in catastrophic decline, some disappearing entirely from the land between one assessment study and the next. The reindeer in Siberia are suffering not only from the deadly combination of climate change and the energy industry, but also from mass slaughter by poachers who are brutally removing the animal's velvet-covered antlers to sell to the Chinese traditional medicine market.

In Canada, scientists have declared that the endangered woodland caribou present "the greatest terrestrial conservation challenge in North America." The vast tracts of intact boreal forest that provide the food and shelter caribou need to survive are disappearing. Canada clear-cuts one million acres of this critical habitat every year, a significant percentage of it for toilet paper. This in spite of the fact that the boreal forest is the largest source of fresh water in the country and the lungs of the northern hemisphere, producing much of the air we breathe and influencing climate patterns and temperature.

Is the sun setting on wild caribou populations? Let's do what we can to preserve this incredible symbol of our north!

Efforts to preserve this essential wilderness have been met with indifference from the nation's industry, which continues to harvest timber at an unsustainable rate, shrinking and fragmenting caribou habitats and pushing the animals farther and farther north. Loss of an umbrella species like caribou would signal the destabilization of the entire ecosystem, indicating a significant reduction of plant and animal biodiversity with concurrent threats to air quality and clean water sources.

In the current climate change crisis, the importance of the boreal forest is greater than ever before. It covers one of the largest carbon stores on the planet. Protecting this critical habitat is not only essential to the survival of many species, including caribou, but would also align the Canadian government with its commitment to reduce greenhouse gases.

The boreal forest is a living buffer from the impending dangers of global warming. The presence of caribou and efforts for the preservation of the western woodland herds due to their endangered designation and the corresponding legal obligations to conserve their habitat are, in many cases, the only factors preventing the wholesale plunder of this extraordinary biome. Pressures from Canada's industry to exploit the resources of the boreal forest, without regard for the impact on future generations of humans and caribou, puts us all at great risk.

Logging and forest access roads dissecting caribou country offer easier access to the herds by predators such as wolves. These access points, where caribou overwinter, should be closed during that season.

The steep declines in woodland caribou populations have conservation groups and Indigenous peoples scrambling to somehow rescue endangered herds stranded in potentially doomed pockets of old-growth forest. Landscape fragmentation by logging companies has altered the predator-prey dynamics of the ecosystem. Every road pushed through intact caribou habitats provides predators with easy access into the herds' safe zones. As the landscape continues to be degraded by extractive industries, moose and deer move into these cleared areas, attracting wolves, which are their natural predators. The collateral damage inflicted on caribou herds by these four-legged hunters is simply unsustainable.

Scientists believe that relying solely on habitat protection and recovery will ultimately fail these vulnerable sub-herds. The extent of forest destruction is such that in the time needed for the land to regenerate, we will have lost most animals. Research shows that a number of emergency measures used in combination with each other can temporarily stabilize or reverse population declines.

Caribou maternity pens are being constructed as part of the recovery plan for small, fragile herds of mountain caribou in southern and central British Columbia. The strategy of capturing maternal females in the winter and protecting them in enclosures until the calves are 3–5 weeks old appears to be having success.

Reducing the number of moose, deer and wolves in sensitive caribou areas is also being employed as part of this multipronged approach, although this treatment remains controversial. Maternity pens may buy us some precious time as we wait for meaningful legislation that should have been passed years ago, when caribou were designated a threatened species. Some jurisdictions are hastily throwing up fencing around functionally extinct remnants of decimated herds, in a PR ploy to avoid taking responsibility for ignoring years of warnings from scientists. Ultimately, these interventions are only meaningful if they occur within the context of habitat restoration. The long-term objective for caribou populations is to make them self-sustaining.

In June 2020, the United Nations officially confirmed the highest temperature ever recorded in the Arctic. In a Russian town 115 kilometers north of the Arctic

Warming summer temperatures are delaying the season's final freeze-up across much of the north, keeping waterways open longer in autumn and earlier in spring, which can result in more challenging crossings.

Increasing temperatures in the Far North will have significant impact on caribou.

Circle, the thermometer reached a scorching 100.4°F (38°C). In North America, summer temperatures in the Arctic have also broken heat records, remaining above 60°F (15.5°C) into October and delaying final freeze-up by a month or more.

In caribou habitats, these new weather patterns are promoting the rapid growth of woody vegetation that is inferior forage for caribou, who need an abundance of protein-rich sedges and flowering plants. Tundra greening is happening earlier in the spring to the extent that by the time the maternal herd arrives at the calving area, the plants have grown past their foraging prime, resulting in overall reduced forage quality for caribou later in the summer. In addition, a warming planet means a dangerous increase in the numbers of biting bugs that torment caribou and a longer season of insect harassment. This will certainly impact maternal health, the most important indicator for calf survival.

The ice freezing later and to a lesser depth in the Far North also physically inhibits the movement of caribou to their wintering grounds, as they are instinctively afraid

A herd of caribou in the snow during their annual migration, near Goose Bay, Labrador, Canada. If ice forms a thick crust on the snow, it can prevent caribou from accessing their food.

PHOTO CREDIT: NIGEL BEAN/MINDEN PICTURES

Continual declines in several barren-ground caribou populations have Indigenous groups and conservation organizations sounding the alarm bells.

of new, thin ice and will delay crossings. Off the northern coast of Canada and Alaska, the Arctic Ocean and Chukchi Sea have become completely ice-free for extended periods, even in winter, leading to more evaporation, increased precipitation in the form of rainstorms and many more ice-on-snow events.

When ice forms in a thick crust over the ground, caribou may find it hard or impossible to break through to reach lichen or their preferred vegetation. Caribou and reindeer herds all around the Arctic Circle are experiencing the climate change-induced dangers of thaw-freeze events, some leading to mass starvation.

In winter 2019, over 60,000 reindeer belonging to herders in Siberia perished because the ice crust covering their forage was too thick for the animals to break through. Global warming is altering the winter ranges of caribou and reindeer from a cold and dry environment to one that is wet and mild, bringing with it the specter of mass caribou die-offs.

In the last five years, changes in the numbers and behavior of the large migratory herds of barren-ground caribou have Indigenous groups and conservationists around the world sounding alarm bells. The movement of herds has become unpredictable and perilous due to the structural and vegetative changes in the landscape that they roam. Decreasing ice formation means caribou are confronted with much more open water and expend precious energy going around lakes or swimming across fast-flowing rivers that were previously frozen when the migrating herds crossed.

An increase in violent storms has accelerated the erosion of riverbanks and beaches, making the terrain more hazardous and difficult to navigate. These changes are compounding to delay migration, significantly altering traditional routes and directly impacting the fecundity of the caribou by reducing the condition of maternal females.

In Canada, extreme heat was a key factor in fueling the devastating wildfires in British Columbia that burned nearly 8,700 square kilometers of land in 2021. The increase in wildfire activity is undermining the resiliency of the evergreen trees which dominate North America's boreal forests. Dense stands of black spruce provide shelter and harbor ground lichen mats and tree lichens, the major forage for caribou in winter.

Drier conditions in the long term lead away from black spruce dominance, and shorter, more intense fire cycles are destroying these conifers before they can reach reproductive maturity. Fire events seriously fragment caribou habitats, as the animals naturally avoid burn areas, which are mostly devoid of lichens and leave caribou exposed to predators.

The remains of a majestic bull from the protected barren-ground herd in Denali National Park and Preserve, Alaska.

Modern technology is helping researchers accurately report on the status and condition of both caribou and their habitat in remote locations. Drones make vegetation surveys more efficient, collecting high-resolution photos and video for further analysis. They can scan the terrain and help map plant matter to understand how much caribou food exists in the area. Drones, unlike planes, can fly unobtrusively above herds, taking a real-time census and recording the animals' condition.

Large accredited zoos are not waiting for the outcomes of many inadequate, last-ditch efforts to save endangered animal populations from extinction and have made serious investments in the cryopreservation of disappearing wildlife DNA, including that of caribou. For over a decade, Dr. Gabriela Mastromonaco, the

Dr. Gabriela Mastromonaco, director of conservation science at the Toronto Zoo, is shown working on the cryogenic biobank that stores reproductive material for some endangered caribou herds.

PHOTO CREDIT: PILI PALM-LEIS

director of conservation science at the Toronto Zoo in Ontario, Canada, has advocated for the collection of reproductive material from caribou to be stored in cryogenic biobanks as a safety net to secure genetic diversity should we fail to stem the tide of extirpation within the species.

After 13 years of research with the University of Saskatchewan, the Toronto Zoo announced in December 2021 that four wood bison, a threatened species that remain only in northwest Canada, were now pregnant with female embryos, proving that advanced reproductive techniques, such as insemination with sex-sorted sperm, work with wildlife. This breakthrough has huge implications for boosting the proportion of female calves in conservation herds and could potentially augment populations of endangered caribou.

"Reproductive technologies such as AI [artificial insemination] and in vitro fertilization are important tools for improving genetic management and connectivity of small populations," says Mastromonaco as we tour the zoo's cryogenic lab. She opens a tank of liquid nitrogen and pulls out a canister of canes full of sperm straws, each holding 20 million sperm — enough for one insemination. She is hoping that the collection of DNA becomes an integral part of baseline conservation procedure as caribou are collared for research.

"Catheterizing males and drawing semen takes five additional minutes," she says. Collecting female reproductive material is trickier, but "First Nations hunters can easily remove the ovaries at the time that a caribou is harvested." The involvement of Indigenous communities is key to the preservation of caribou herds, and interested members could be instructed on how to handle and ship tissue samples.

Her team is not just preserving gametes and embryos. Animal skin cells can be easily grown in cultures and reprogrammed to become eggs and sperm, and the Toronto Zoo plans to extend their biobanks to include these fibroblast samples. The future of caribou biodiversity may well be in the hands of these visionary conservation scientists, and zoological societies have an important role to play in preventing endangered DNA from disappearing.

A radio-collared cow of the mountain caribou herd in northern British Columbia, Canada.
PHOTO CREDIT: ERIC BREWER

Opposite: A female woodland caribou follows a path through the boreal forest — an ecosystem worth protecting.

A bull of the critically endangered mountain caribou herd of the Tonquin Valley in Jasper National Park, Alberta.
PHOTO CREDIT: SIMONE HEINRICH

As diminished herds, one by one, tip from functional extirpation into oblivion in real time, caribou have become the flashpoint of conflicting interests between conservationists and natural-resource economies. Many herds in Canada have seen a 90 percent decline in the last 30 years, and many mountain groups in British Columbia and Alberta are down to less than that.

Caribou subgroups are disappearing yearly, if not monthly. Their teetering populations and the inaction of parks and governments have forced scientists and conservation groups to consider whether bureaucrats might be reluctant to follow up on their urgent recommendations to stave off a mass caribou extinction because it would be so much easier if the herds continued their precipitous decline and went away altogether.

Preserving the most endangered caribou populations requires emergency orders at the federal level to protect and regenerate large tracts of old-growth forest that the woodland subspecies simply cannot live without.

It requires that the vast pristine peat lands that mining companies have prematurely riddled with claims remain largely undisturbed, not just because of the endangered herds of caribou they shelter, but because peat lands sequester huge amounts of carbon and methane.

It requires restricting human activities such as heli-skiing in high-quality caribou wintering habitats and seasonally closing roads and trails that give wolves easy access to the animals in their safest spaces. And it requires facing the truth that, given all of the alternatives at the disposal of policy makers, there is no excuse for precipitating extinction.

The climate change emergency is a caribou emergency. In mitigating one, we mitigate the other. If there are healthy, stable populations of caribou on the planet, then hundreds of other species of plants and animals that share their habitat are also in good shape, including us.

Let's do what we can to help these magnificent animals continue to roam freely across the wild north.

Opposite: The unparalleled majesty of a barren-ground bull.

What will the future hold for the wild caribou populations of North America? A caribou calf stares out over the ocean at sunset. Our greatest wish is that this is a "red sky at night" moment for this amazing species.

PHOTOGRAPHING CARIBOU

The surprise and spontaneity of wildlife photography is one of the reasons it's perennially fascinating. My son Andrew and I were on a two-week adventure, camping, hiking and photographing the wildlife in the vast backcountry of Denali National Park and Preserve. A truly wild and magnificent landscape in the interior of Alaska, each trip there has been a tremendous privilege and provided its own rare experiences.

Andrew and I set out from our camp shortly after daybreak with plans to hike and scan for wildlife from the surrounding hilltops. This expansive region is mostly open country, but it is also very hilly, and caribou, moose, wolves and grizzlies can easily be out of sight in the undulating terrain.

Our camera backpacks were full of gear, including water, a water filter, food (mostly power bars), extra wool underlayers, a raincoat outer shell, a headlamp and more, in preparation for a day on the tundra. As a precaution, we also each carried a can of bear spray, as we frequently saw grizzly bears sharing the grand landscape.

Andrew photographs an Alaskan barren-ground caribou bull as it walks along a ridge in the fiery glory of autumn.

141

We were in search of a tremendous bull moose that a friend of mine had glimpsed while camping in the area — a bull that I was familiar with. I'd photographed him two years before, and he was now featured on the cover of my moose book. Based on my friend's photo, this bull moose had grown to be a crowned giant!

The call of migrating sandhill cranes kept us company as hundreds of birds circled above, seemingly discussing the migratory plan for the day, or maybe how to best pass over or around the daunting Alaska Range — the tallest on the continent.

Andrew and I methodically hiked and glassed from one vantage point to another, following, as best we could, the game trails used by countless animals over the centuries to crisscross this wilderness landscape. For the first couple of hours, we didn't spot anything wearing a hide. But as we peeked over the third colorful rise, our eyes widened with excitement at the sight of a pair of mature caribou bulls — at close range!

One of the bulls pauses during feeding in a stunning autumn scene.

We watched for a few minutes as they fed in the nearby valley, 200 yards from us. As we crested the hilltop to begin a descent, they froze and stared, unsure at first.

But each time they looked at us, we'd stop walking and look away, seemingly disinterested. This gentle approach helped them to settle back into feeding, while also giving us an excuse to grab a couple of handfuls of the delicious wild blueberries that carpeted the tundra.

Direct eye contact can be a powerful thing, especially when advancing on a prey species like caribou. I always avoid looking directly at their face until it's clear that they've accepted our presence.

After 20 minutes, the animals realized that we weren't a threat and allowed us to be within 50 yards of them to photograph them in the kaleidoscope of autumn color. It was a breathtaking scene! We spent the next couple of hours in their company as they moved and fed from one spot to another. Eventually we'd traveled far enough with the handsome pair that we decided we'd better make our way back to camp.

We never spotted the moose of our original intent, but we did have one of our most memorable days as a father-and-son team. The photographic opportunities that unfolded in the overcast light on the expansive autumn tundra with the caribou were more than enough cause for celebration!

From my very first time photographing caribou — what a day. I'm grateful for the experience and the memory.

My career as a wildlife photographer began in my early 20s. I was completing my degree in wildlife biology at the University of Guelph in Ontario, Canada, and had begun working on field research on white-tailed deer.

I had enjoyed taking photos of animals throughout my teens, but I never realized that it could be a profession, nor did I ever own suitable equipment. It was during my research that I met some wildlife photographers who were as eagerly searching for deer as I was. In my spare time, I helped them to locate the deer, and in turn they shared their experience as professionals in the field.

To me, the idea of being able to immerse oneself in the wilderness, to observe, learn and document wildlife, was irresistible. I continued with more fieldwork, focusing on white-tailed deer populations, and with the aid of some used

Mark in his happy place! Moving at nature's pace and working in the elements.

professional camera gear (it really does make a big difference!), my portfolio began to grow. Within a year, I began submitting images to magazines.

Like most of my colleagues in this profession, I didn't have any formal photography schooling. I educated myself on composition by studying magazines and analyzing the work of those who were successfully publishing. The camera became a tool that was like an extension of myself. There was a lot of trial and error, and many disappointments along the way, but the reward of creating the desired image was more than enough to fuel my perseverance.

It's essential to understand a camera's settings, but when it comes to wildlife photography, I consider it to be even more relevant to success to understand the animals themselves. Knowledge of their behavior and biology is essential to be able to predict what they might do next in order to be in the best position to capture the most striking visuals.

Documenting behavior is one of the most challenging and fulfilling goals of a wildlife photographer. Building a decent portfolio on a species that we're passionate

about requires significant time, effort and patience. Such a collection of work allows us not only to share these wonderful experiences with others, but also to educate and spark interest in a species and the environment that they inhabit. One of the most exciting aspects of creating a caribou book is the hope that it can advocate for and inspire others to appreciate this remarkable animal. Pili and I have come to love caribou, and we treasure the opportunity to spend time in their company. We are eager to share why they've grown on us so much and why now, more than ever, we need to care about this species and the land they depend on to survive. We hope that you will check out and expand your interest in caribou and the Far North by looking up some of the relevant links (and their QR codes) that we've included at the back of this book.

Filming a video of a beautiful bull that approached and fed past our position during the autumn post-rut.

I love the connection and focus created when an animal approaches the camera (a large 500mm telephoto in this case). The water droplets and raised front hoof make this a favorite dynamic image.

Photography equipment is advancing at a mind-blowing pace. The emergence of larger sensors, faster processors, advanced autofocus (AF) animal eye-tracking capabilities and in-camera stabilization in the latest generation of mirrorless cameras all continue to expand what we can accomplish in the field. Mirrorless cameras are smaller, lighter and, yes, silent. No flapping mirror can make a big difference in the wild. The sound of the mirror never really bothered me; it was a good sound, it meant success and that images were being collected. After using mirrorless cameras for six weeks in the wilderness, I picked up my DSLR and the sound of the mirror … well, let's just say that I don't miss it.

For the past several years, I've been using a Nikon D850 camera with a Nikon 200-500mm f/5.6 lens and absolutely loved the results. The stabilization capabilities of this lens allowed for handheld operation with exceptional sharpness. This camera also boasts a decently high ISO (the equivalent of film speed), especially compared to the old days of slide film, which was limited to an ISO of 50–200 for the best quality.

Even with these technological advancements, I currently prefer to cap my ISO at 800 or less, but I will bump it to 1,000 when necessary, and as high as 1,600 if there's some behavior in low light that must be captured. Further improvements in ISO are something that I eagerly anticipate as cameras evolve. The ability to photograph wildlife in the low light of dawn or dusk is very important, as many species are most active at these times. Thankfully, caribou are active throughout the day as well, providing plenty of photographic opportunities. The challenge is to locate them after a night of continual wandering.

When photographing caribou, I prefer to use a zoom lens. Why? It's actually a big deal! A telephoto zoom lens allows me to quickly change compositions and collect a variety of images without moving much. The less I move, the less attention the animals will pay to me and the more they will follow their natural pattern of interaction with the land and one another, which I'll be able to document.

I no longer use a tripod when collecting still images. Why not? First, there's the weight of carrying it for miles and miles across the tundra. Second, there's the fact that the stabilization capabilities of most modern cameras can consistently create tack sharp images without a tripod. And third, I can quickly make micro-adjustments to the composition (as the animals are often moving) by leaning a few inches one way or the other, which would be impossible to do rapidly when anchored to a tripod.

When recording video, we do work with a tripod to ensure smooth footage. The lone exception is short clips of action that can happen spontaneously — like when two bulls suddenly begin sparring, or one animal chases another, and I must quickly record the sequence.

This is when we rely on the capabilities of the most up-to-date cameras. They have an advantage by having both IBIS (the acronym for "in-body image stabilization") and stabilization in the lens to help create smooth, stable video without any shaking. This is why I pur-

One of the most photogenic barren-ground caribou that I have ever photographed.

chased a new mirrorless Canon EOS R5 camera this year with the impressively compact Canon RF 100–500mm f/4.5–7.1 IS USM lens. For those wondering how powerful this lens is, a 500mm lens is equivalent to 10 times magnification. The small size and weight of this kit (pack weight is a game-changer when we hike for days), coupled with its advanced animal-eye autofocus function, makes this combo a perfect wilderness kit.

It's not just the most modern cameras and lenses that are worth mentioning; I must also highlight the impressive capabilities of ever-evolving image software such as Adobe Photoshop and Lightroom. This is not to suggest that a photograph should ever be changed in ways that most wildlife photographers would consider unethical. We never make significant visual changes to the animal; it's more about correctly adjusting the colors, contrast, brightness, horizon level and framing of the image.

All serious photographers that I know shoot in RAW file format. This offers the most latitude for adjustment. If one were to shoot in JPEG file format in the field,

A striking image of a woodland caribou stag on the barrens of Newfoundland at "golden hour." A favorite photographic scenario of mine!

it would vastly reduce their ability to work on an image post-production, as JPEG files can only be re-saved a few times before deteriorating. This is not the case with RAW files.

As you can imagine, collecting images in the field is by far the most gratifying part of the job, but for the best results with digital photography, significant work at the computer with a properly color-calibrated monitor is required.

When are the best times of the year to photograph caribou? Aside from documenting some seasonal behaviors, large mammals like caribou don't look their best all year long. Their coats change color, and they also molt seasonally. But from midsummer through to winter, they are very photogenic. My favorite time to be afield with them is from early autumn through to winter. They are at their annual peak physical condition during this time of year, and there are virtually no biting insects — which can be a really big deal on the tundra! Their environment also looks great throughout autumn, as fall colors can create stunning visuals. Early September is my favorite time to be in Alaska or the Yukon to hopefully witness velvet shedding with the brilliant red foliage, whereas mid-October is my choice time for woodland caribou in Newfoundland, because it's the rut, and the tamarack trees turn a brilliant gold color, creating a stunning backdrop. Cool fact: tamaracks are conifers that shed their needles annually.

Here are a couple of quick tips to up your photography game. First, work in good light. What is good light? This is a critical baseline for quality images. Good light on sunny days occurs during the first and last three hours of the day. As the sun drops lower in the sky, it creates softer light at an angle where it's easier to capture the catchlight in the animal's eye. The first and last hour of a sunny day is affectionately called the "golden hour" by photographers due to the incredible richness of light.

148

The middle portion of a cloudless day typically offers poor light for nature photography, as it is too harsh with the sun directly overhead, resulting in stark shadows. But if it's a cloudy day, the sunlight is filtered and softened, often to the point where there are no shadows — and that means game on! Overcast conditions allow for photography all day and is a favorite for autumn colors.

Next, watch the background of the image. It's easy to miss distracting branches or objects that can create unwanted lines or bright contrasts in the heat of the moment, but these can distract the viewer's eye away from the subject.

Capturing action images is always desirable. When an animal is running, chasing another animal, sparring or swimming, we must make sure that the shutter speed is fast enough to stop the movement. A minimum of 1/500 of a second is desired, and higher than that if possible.

Environmental portraits that show an animal as a small portion of the world that it inhabits have become very popular in recent years. These scenic images can be created without being near the animal.

A mature woodland caribou stag along the coast of Newfoundland.

The newest cameras with animal-eye autofocus help when a subject is running straight on. This herd bull was chasing an adolescent male away from the female.

For images highlighting the animal's physique and specific behaviors, it is essential to be closer — typically, less than 50 yards. I have to be careful doing this with some large North American mammals such as moose or elk, but caribou usually aren't as aggressive during the rut. That being said, I always keep an eye on the herd bull and the contenders orbiting around him.

When it comes to appealing compositions, practicing the rule of thirds is a great place to start. This is where you imagine a tic-tac-toe grid that divides up your frame. Some new cameras can be programmed to place this in your viewfinder — personally, I'd find it too distracting. By imagining this grid, it encourages us to position the subject not in the middle of the frame but rather off to the right or left third of the image, leaving the other two-thirds in front of the primary subject. Positioning the subject off to the upper or lower right or left side where the lines cross in the grid makes an appealing composition.

You can also adjust for this in post-processing on the computer by cropping — especially with the newer 45-megapixel and larger sensor cameras that produce large file sizes.

Another tip is to be at or below the animal's eye level whenever it's possible and safe to do so. This generally makes for a superior image than photographing from above, as the animal will look more majestic.

Timing the catchlight in the animal's eye is also essential to taking appealing images — this brings the subject to life.

Silhouettes are one of my favorite visuals for storytelling. Silhouettes create a mood and imply an action, while leaving something to the imagination of the viewer. The light is dramatic, but not all of the details are visible, creating a more

mysterious image. And they are so much fun to create! It's helpful that caribou inhabit a relatively open landscape where they can be framed against the skyline.

I'll frequently lie down on the comfortable tundra to pull this off. I begin just as the sun touches the horizon and continue to well after sunset. To the naked eye, the sky may or may not look vibrant, but when you underexpose the photograph by a full stop or two, or more, it becomes increasingly striking. The oranges and reds pop to create a very satisfying image. If there are streaks of clouds, it can be even more dramatic. So the day doesn't necessarily end as the sun sets when photographing caribou.

It's obvious that the best camera gear is of utmost importance to create professional-caliber images. But to be truthful, none of that happens in caribou country without proper footwear. Having the best boots possible for the job can make or break days of hiking mile upon mile on the tundra. My philosophy is to

Making the animal smaller in an image to highlight their habitat creates an environmental portrait. Here, a regal barren-ground caribou bull is shown in his home — the foothills of the Alaska Range.

invest in the best possible boots and buy them less often than if I'd gone a cheaper route. Success, comfort and safety (including ankle support) start at the feet on the tundra.

To wrap up this book on this iconic species of the north, here's a window into one of the best days that we spent in caribou country this year.

Darkness still loomed outside the cabin as we sipped coffee and prepared our gear. Surprisingly, the perennial gale-force winds that often blow on the edge of the Newfoundland tundra had fallen silent. We could be in for a spectacular day!

We layered up and headed outdoors in hopes of finding caribou sooner rather than later, to capture the pre-sunrise silhouettes of their elegant antlers against a red sky. It had yet to snow, but the frost crystals blinked across the landscape. As the last stars of night began to fade into the increasingly orange-colored sky, we made our way along the same route that we'd followed for the past week. We rounded a hilltop to catch sight of a group of moose moving along the nearby shoreline. I pointed my camera, and at this distance zoomed

almost to 500mm to record the group silhouetted against the water. After a few quick frames, I realized that the scene would be improved if I actually zoomed the lens back a bit to include the hills across the narrow bay. I was so focused, trying to properly expose and bracket the predawn scene, that I didn't notice that we had another visitor moving nearby.

Pili touched my shoulder and motioned off to the left. Wow! A dramatically colored cross fox was slowly hunting and making its way along the tuckamore evergreen shrubs a mere 40 yards from us! We stood and watched it scouting along the line of brush, as it was simply too dark to do anything else. What are the odds that we'd see this striking color morph of a red fox? I've only encountered them on two other occasions in 25 years! That's when we began silently pleading that it would hang around for another 15 minutes or so. Just a bit more time, and the rising sun was sure to brighten enough for pic-

I'd be happy to begin every day with a view like this! A bull moose moves along the shoreline at sunrise.

tures. It felt like an eternity. But good fortune was on our side, and the sly animal remained in the area. It even sat down for a spell and watched us, almost like it was waiting for its photo op as well. As the sun rose, I finally was able to collect a handful of images of this beautiful animal before its curiosity waned and it trotted off and out of sight. In my mind, the day was already a success! That was such a rare sighting. As the sun rose above the horizon, the moose moved off into a patch of forest for the day, and we were back to wondering where the caribou might be. Would we find them in the next few hours to make use of the morning light?

Looking about with our binoculars, we could see no sign of the brown-and-white animals.

We had a cell signal in this area and, with a limited time for good photography light, chose the "divide and conquer" option, splitting up to scout the taiga.

Opposite, top & bottom: The sun sets over the ocean as a mature stag approaches a female during the October rut.

After an hour of hiking and 2 kilometers later, I received a text from Pili. She'd found them! A group of 17 woodland caribou. The only problem was, they were over 2 kilometers from my position, and the light was intensifying by the minute. But that wasn't all. She texted that they were heading toward a cove, and she had a feeling they would swim it. After hearing that, there was no longer any need for caffeine in my system! Could this be the day? You see, there's been an image in my mind for a long time, a dream of witnessing and photographing a herd of caribou swimming in open water in good light. Visions of the white animals embedded in cobalt-blue water, creating a dramatic contrast, and the big stag's rack of antlers as he swam chin-deep in the ocean filled my mind.

"Hurry!" she said. "I'll try!" I replied, already making a beeline toward her position.

The striking cross fox pauses on the frost-covered tundra at daybreak.

I'd race-walked about 500 yards when, almost right underfoot, up popped a super-photogenic willow ptarmigan! This bird was in mid-molt, meaning its feathers were a beautiful collage of brown and white. Place that against the background of the ocean, as I was on top of a bluff, and what a picture that would be! The caribou would have to wait. I photographed the tolerant bird for about 10 minutes as it fed and walked across the barren. I thanked it and almost ran across the rough ground toward the caribou.

I tried to text Pili for an update, but the signal was lost. All I could do was continue on and push through the fatigue. I worked my way down the bluff, closer to the shoreline, as I covered the final kilometer. At one point, I glanced up and saw two female caribou about 500 yards ahead. A good sign, but they quickly turned and walked out of sight toward the cove. "Oh, man," I said to myself. "Keep going! If they swim — there's no guarantee — you can't miss that in this light! That would be a crushing disappointment."

I managed to crest the last rise, and finally I saw the main herd. They were still about 200 yards ahead and only 100 yards from the water's edge. With tremendous relief, I hiked past them to get on the right side of the light. I caught up with Pili, and we continued on, looking for the place where the caribou would be able to work their way through the boulders strewn on the shoreline and find the shortest distance to swim across the channel.

We'd lost sight of the herd to climb down and to be in position, if they actually decided to continue on and swim across.

As soon as I made it to the water's edge, I looked up and was both shocked and amazed to see a single-file group of bobbing heads already swimming through the ocean swells about 150 yards away — almost where we'd left them! Somehow we'd missed the access trail they used to reach the water's edge and had hiked to the next one.

The beautiful mid-molt plumage of this tolerant willow ptarmigan was a delight to photograph on the barrens.

My mind raced, as it was now or never to get the shot. I quickly race-walked along the rocky beach, navigating boulders and slippery surfaces to try to close the gap as much as I dared before they swam too much of the channel. *This would have to do!* I raised my camera and zoomed in on the confidently swimming herd and held the shutter button down. I still get excited thinking about that moment. It was a dream come true to witness it, and even more so to document it in that spectacular light. By lunchtime, I'd experienced my most memorable day as a wildlife photographer for the year. Thank you, caribou!

We hope that this book has offered an exciting portal into the natural history of these remarkable animals and the incredible region of the planet that they call home.

The goal! The dream! The result of being able to document the behavior of the caribou swimming across the cove in the beautiful morning light made it all worthwhile!

CARIBOU RANGE

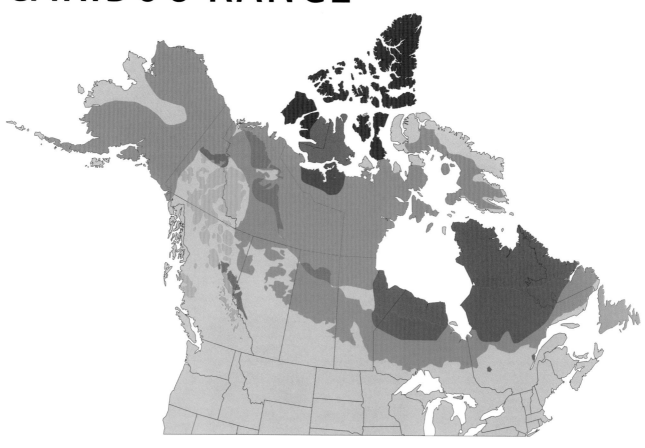

Peary
Endangered

Dolphin and Union
Endangered

Dolphin and Union / Barren-Ground overlap

Barren-Ground
Threatened

Boreal / Barren-Ground overlap

Boreal
Threatened

Northern Mountain
Threatened

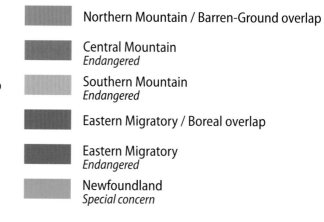

Northern Mountain / Barren-Ground overlap

Central Mountain
Endangered

Southern Mountain
Endangered

Eastern Migratory / Boreal overlap

Eastern Migratory
Endangered

Newfoundland
Special concern

INDEX

Page numbers in *italic* represent photos.